To Dick Dopp
from our mutual friend
Chester Taylor

with all The best
Hakan Toyfor

The Gift of the Refugees

Other Books

by Hakon Torjesen
The House Husband:
Reflections on a Changing World

by Karen Olness, M.D.
Parenting Happy Healthy Children
Practical Pediatrics
in Less-Developed Countries

The Gift of the Refugees

Notes of a Volunteer Family at a Refugee Camp

Hakon Torjesen
Karen Olness M.D.
Erik Torjesen

THE GARDEN
Eden Prairie, Minnesota

Published by The Garden
6605 Rowland Road, Eden Prairie, Minnesota 55344, USA

ISBN 0-9602790-3-2
Library of Congress Catalog Card #81-81082

First Printing, March, 1981
Printed in the United States of America

To
Chansamone

Contents

Foreword

Gretchen Quie

The shifting of populations of people from one continent to another has enormous consequences for both sides. Many of us are the products of earlier waves of emigration from want and misery in search of a better life. Today, refugees from the upheavals in Southeast Asia are crowding the camps in Thailand, and looking for new beginnings.

In the United States, as well as in other countries, we accept many of these refugees with open arms. We do so because we believe it is the compassionate way to respond. Yet, we have misgivings. We wonder how they will fit in, find jobs, learn the language? Will they bring strange diseases and crime? We have to remind ourselves that, just as Jesus taught us "it is more blessed to give than to receive," so we are quite likely to be the greater beneficiaries in the long run for having welcomed the refugees. We give them a new homeland and our caring. They give us, as this book so vividly demonstrates, the strongest, most clever and most self-sufficient members of their population. They give us people who, like our forefathers, have encountered adversity and have survived.

It is a fascinating and wonderful experience that Hakon, Karen, Erik, Kristine, Malika, and Mark share on these pages. Here is an American family, children and all, fighting disease and desperation in Thailand, and discovering in the refugees the "Giants in the Earth" of the 1980's. This is not a romantic vision. It is drawn from five months of a family's actual experience of living and working with Lao refugees in Thailand. They encountered death, disease, starvation and despair. But they discovered an incredibly optimistic people, who, "like the bamboo stalk that bends with the wind," have survived the storm and will continue to grow.

When we try to help newly-arrived refugees, we often know very little about their former life, and what they are thinking and feeling. This book, by opening the door on the life of a group of refugees in their former culture, is a rich source of insight into their adaptation in our country.

I marvel at the examples here of how to live, work, and communicate with people in another culture, how to give health care when you lack almost all the modern trappings of the trade, and how to focus, amid daily emergencies, on long-term goals such as nutrition and sanitation. I marvel, too, at the rich experience the teenagers had in helping other human beings, and in taking on projects that would tax the ingenuity of adults.

Here in Minnesota, and throughout our nation, we are blessed in that we have the capacity for sending volunteer families overseas, and receiving refugee families into our communities, and helping them get started. We even have the capacity, most of the time, for recognizing the gift of the refugees. For the thousands of us—volunteers and professionals, here at home and overseas—who work with refugees, this book is a gift of practical experience, and a gift of inspiration.

Gretchen Quie
The Governor's Residence
St. Paul

PART
ONE

A Day at Nongkhai

1
Monday Morning Hakon

It's four-thirty—that morning interval before a hot April sun in Thailand when you can actually bear to pull a cover over you. Karen is stirring. She mutters something about the baby girl . . . died yesterday . . . malnourished, but no formula was given Sunday at the hospital. I move closer, and drift back to sleep.

At six-thirty we jog around the house. Today it's Karen and I; more often it would be she and Erik. I brew a pot of stateside coffee, an American habit that has refused to die in the months here. Then comes the crescendo of four children stumbling to life, and chores, and planning of the day.

Karen pulls out the typewriter for a few letters before the ride to camp . . . one to the Australian Embassy about a Lao refugee family, whose six-month-old shows signs of a severe metabolic disease that will need sophisticated evaluation . . . and another medical case for the American resettlement authorities.

The morning plan has evolved. Erik, aged fourteen, will work at home on the summary of last year's hospital records. The girls, Kristine and Malika, aged thirteen and twelve, will cover the hospital day care center this morning, and Mark, aged eleven, will help the volunteers at Food for the Hungry. Karen has hospital rounds, I have errands, and at ten-thirty we will go to town to try to spring from the city jail a refugee father whose malnourished baby is fighting for life on the hospital ward.

As we load into the pickup, we are talking about the book. What can we do on that manuscript in the last month here? We need an opening theme! Maybe we should do a typical day? Maybe today?

The four-mile drive to the camp is never routine. The road is excellent, constructed as a dike. But all who use it seem to lay exclusive claim to it. The clear winner in this game is the water buffalo. He alone can bring a massive rig of teak logs to a screeching halt. The Thai have fondly dubbed him "the inspector general" of the highway. Foreign drivers can be equally unnerved by the claims of everything from buses to *samlars* (three-wheel pedal-powered taxis), plus dogs and pedestrians and the latest import—joggers. Today we are missing our favorite incongruity, the exercise buff who finds the smooth pavement just right for a meditative head-stand.

The Lao Refugee Camp, the *Soon*, as the Thai and the Lao call it, sits on about 200 acres of flat land on the eastern outskirts of Nongkhai, and about a mile south of the Mekong river. Across the Mekong river bed, itself only about a mile wide, is Laos, the homeland that the refugees have escaped. Vientiane, the capital of Laos, is located a few miles upstream on the other side.

The guards at the camp barricade wave us in. The Thai,

MAP OF SOUTHEAST ASIA   ●= Refugee Camps

like the Lao, have a distaste for Western rigidness about things like showing your pass at the gate. But, you can never be sure about that gate!

The camp hospital is straight ahead. It survived the fire two months ago that left 20,000 refugees homeless. It sits alone, now, in a gray pool of ashes. Karen and the kids hop off, and I swing back to town.

2
Rounds

Karen

It's eight o'clock. It takes time to get from the pickup to the ward, because people are waiting to pounce. "Will you read this X ray . . . " "My boy has had a fever for two days . . . " "Can you help me get to America . . . " The Lao are masterful interrupters. And they manage it without compromising the grace and delicacy for which they are famed. I try to answer, and press on to the ward.

The hospital is a bare but serviceable wooden structure with two open wards, one for 20 adults, the other for 30 children. The beds are wooden platforms with straw mats on them. Those at one end have new holes cut in the middle. That's an old bush-hospital technique for handling the constant diarrhea of cholera patients. Now that a cholera epidemic is threatening, our need for an isolation ward is critical. The hospital is unscreened, rather dark, but well ventilated. Adjoining the wards are a nursing station and small emergency and delivery rooms. Across the alley is the OPD—the outpatient department—and a small laboratory and pharmacy. There is a staff of about thirty refugee medical people and a dozen or more expatriates.

The MIHV (Minnesota International Health Volunteers) team here consists of two doctors, two nurses, and two medical students, plus family members, on rotations of three to six months. We are supported by the International Rescue Committee (IRC), which coordinates the medical work here, by the American Refugee Committee (ARC), and by clubs, churches, and other contributors at home. In addition to our health services, MIHV does teaching and clinical research related to international health.

I start pediatric rounds with Bob Bidwell, one of our medical students. Soon we are joined by a Lao nurse, and by Bounma, the former teacher who does the feeding on the ward. Both Bob and I speak some Lao. The patients are cordial.

The first, second and third patients we see have diarrhea with dehydration. Cholera? This test was ordered Saturday! Why aren't the cultures done yet? The nurses don't know. They weren't here yesterday. Nobody knows.

At the next bed we present two old dresses and three panties to an eight-year-old orphan girl with severe pneumonia. The girl and the *Mhae Thao* (elderly lady) who is her protector both beam. I know they are very poor. She will need a chest X ray at the Nongkhai hospital, and she can ride in with us at ten-thirty. I tell them to be ready. A little later the *Mhae Thao* calls me back and the girl presents me with a fresh mango. I hate to accept what to them is a valuable gift, but I must. I *wai* my thanks by bringing my palms together on my chest. She *wais* in return, dangling her IV (intravenous feeding) tube from one hand.

We move on to the severely malnourished four-month-old boy, whose father is in the Nongkhai prison. He has been there six months waiting for a hearing on a complaint that he was involved in a burglary. The young mother is depressed and has neglected the baby her husband has never seen. Last Saturday we made a deal with her that if she would feed the baby his 40 cc every two hours all weekend, we would take her to town on Monday to see if we could get her husband out. She agreed excitedly. Today she has the prepared look about her, and a friend on hand to watch the baby.

Thanks to Roy Dexter, the prospects for the husband's release are fairly good. Roy is the IRC medical technologist. He learned Thai in the Peace Corps, and has a deeper understanding of our host culture than most expatriates can hope to achieve. On Saturday he visited both the court house and the jail to see what could be done. And he kept an eye all weekend on the mother's end of the bargain. The baby has gained 1.5 kilos since admission, but still looks critical. "Ten-thirty," I say. She nods happily.

The next patient is a new admission, a seven-year-old boy with severe pneumonia. He needs an X ray, so we prepare the requisition and tell him, too, to be ready at ten-thirty.

Then comes the boy whom I resuscitated ten days ago at the detention center (see page 64). He is recovering from meningitis. Approaching the bed, I see that his grandmother is here for the first time. The old lady had been blowing and muttering over the boy's body as I did my mouth-to-mouth resuscitation. We remember each other instantly. Was it her blowing, or my blowing? Only God knows. She bows, and I bow in return. But wait . . . the boy looks feverish again . . . and the IV is out

. . . and no antibiotics for the last 24 hours. I call Jerry, the IRC nurse, and ask her to please keep an eye on this one, and I know there are too many like him for her to watch.

We move on to a boy with a possible glomerulonephritis, complicated by being run over by a *samlar* (pedicab) three weeks ago. Neither we nor the Nongkhai hospital can do the sophisticated diagnostics on a case like this. So we keep him here, and watch him. I remind the father about not giving the boy too much salt, and Bounma reinforces me.

The next patient is a sixteen-month-old boy who has had intermittent bloody urine for several weeks. A bladder stone? That's the most likely reason in this culture. I ask about his diet. He went off milk at seven months. And, yes, his main diet since then has been sticky rice. That's consistent with the pattern clinicians see here. But no one has gotten around to investigating a possible relationship between a steady diet of glutinous rice and the very high incidence of bladder stones in young children.

We rush; it's already nine-thirty. Here are three siblings, all with acute onset diarrhea. Cholera again? Next we see a baby recovering from pneumonia, and one with acute asthma, and another who probably has whooping cough.

There's no oral electrolyte solution left in the pharmacy. That's the news from Doyle Tarwater, the medical student on the OPD side today. What can be done? Can we make some packets? Where is salt and sugar? For that matter, where is water? Bounma is boiling a couple of litres for formulas; but Kevin Dyer is on his three-day weekend. He's the MIHV nurse who, along with doing acute care, has been trying to solve the problem of safe water at the hospital. And in a weekend the plan can collapse.

We examine a screaming two-year-old with giardiasis and malnutrition. His mother wants to take him home, and I'll let her. People stay here only if they want to. Over the weekend two babies with gonorrhea opthalmia disappeared.

We move on to two babies with cholera, in "isolation" at the end of the adult ward. One has begun vomiting blood this morning. I take one look, and see intestinal obstruction. I tell the mother to rush home to her family to say we are transferring the boy to the Nongkhai hospital, and we'll leave in a few minutes. That will be quite a load at ten-thirty. The other cholera patient, aged four months, looks better.

Also on the adult side, a two-year-old malnourished child is sleeping in the bed next to where his mother is dying of an inoperable tumor (see page 105). Usually he whines, so we leave him asleep. We'll come back to him.

We stop to check on Bouahong, the teenage orphan who will have a foster home in the States with David Speert and Sara Lawton. They have just ended their MIHV stint here. He assures us he is taking his anti-tuberculosis drugs. At seven this morning a woman in a near-by bed had died of cholera. I pray he doesn't catch it.

And there is Angie, an IRC nurse from the Philippines, with several Lao nurses, pouring clorox straight from the bottle over some contaminated beds. I like that smell, I say.

"My eyes sting, but I like it too," says Angie.

3

Cascade Hakon

Driving back to town I enjoy a little solitude. No radio, even. Karen, on rounds, will be having the opposite experience. We all have less privacy here than at home. It isn't just our "smaller" house, or even the incredible crowding at the *Soon.* It is knowing that Asia is crowded almost everywhere, and that here, more than at home, a moment alone is to be relished.

First stop is the railway station, where I am making a second try at confirming the schedule for Karen's trip next week to the Thai Medical School at Khon Kaen. This time my Thai is better, or the agent more patient, and we get it straight.

I pause. Just beyond the tracks and the outdoor cafe, I see the Mekong River, glimmering through the overgrowth, and Laos on the other side, less than a mile away. It looks so idyllic for a river where thousands of refugees a month are risking their lives to escape to this side. And it seems unreal that Karen and I had our honeymoon cottage over there, in the sixties, when we were assigned to Laos in the Foreign Service.

Bread Enough

Next stop is the afternoon market. It has done the bulk of a day's business by eight in the morning. But it will stay open all day, and hence its name. As usual, I am one of the few male shoppers at the market. To save time today, I go only to my regular stalls, where the women are accustomed to both my sex and my race.

Under the big roof, I stop first for a half kilo of fresh beansprouts for three *baht* (fifteen cents at the rate of twenty Thai *baht* to one U.S. dollar) and a package of our favorite Chinese soft noodles. Next comes the row of wooden tables on which the meat vendors sit, surrounded by their hunks of pig or buffalo. These girls tend to be more aggressive than the other market women. They call to me, and flash their knives at the pieces they want me to buy.

I head for the only stall where the girl has understood my preference for looking and thinking before she starts cutting and loading the scales. She sells pork. I select one kilo piece, cut from the ribs, that I know will yield a nice set of small filets and enough scraps for several oriental meals. I have wondered why I couldn't find such handy cuts under the celophane at home. Meat is expensive in this economy, but the pricing is simple. It's all forty *baht* a kilo, lean or fat, buffalo or pork. That's about a dollar a pound.

Outside, under one of the umbrellas, the vegetable lady weighs out greens and snow peas and onions. She quells my instinct for bargaining by tossing in a free garlic bulb, a ginger root and a handful of hot peppers. (Just like coupons, I muse.) As usual, she also tries to sell me potatoes. They are "foreign food," and her most expensive item. At thirty cents a pound, we splurge on this favorite only about once a week.

The next stall is newly in business, but I am already a daily customer. Mango season had finally arrived in full force, and here a mother and daughter have five varieties. The price is down now, so I buy the top of the line, a dozen large mangos at two *baht* (ten cents) apiece.

The last stop is for French bread. That Nongkhai should be the home of a superb *baguette* is the happy result of some harsh history—a century of French colonialism in Laos, and then a Communist tyranny that finally drove its bakers across the river. An old refugee started baking the loaf in a charcoal oven right in the *Soon*. It sold there, and then in town, and then local bakers began retaining their own aged masters from the colonial days. Today, bread from the *Soon* at Nongkhai is a delicacy sold all over Northeast Thailand.

As I lug my haul to the truck, I toy with a *potpourri* of thoughts. Who would believe that a community with a dire problem of malnutrition could offer so many of its members the opportunity to eat so luxuriously? On the other hand, if this is so good, why do so many of my fellow expatriates pay stateside prices to crowd the local facsimile of an American greasy spoon? And why, anyway, do markets lose out to supermarkets? But it is too hot a day for answers.

Back home there is water to boil, both to cool for drinking and to pour boiling hot over the dishes to sterilize them (western tricks for avoiding the "Mekong rapids"). I chop the pork scraps and start them frying with ginger and garlic. They will go with noodles and greens at noon, and with rice and greens tonight. Erik has struggled enough with the impossible combination of illegible French, English and Lao entries in the medical records. He has withdrawn to a book. I set the noodles to soak in hot water, and head back to Karen at the Soon.

En route, I stop again at the bank. I was there twice last week, but the telex with money from the states had not yet arrived. Today, when I come in the door, the smiles assure me that our ship is in. Two of our MIHV volunteers have been several days overdue for their $300 a month living allowance. They will soon be smiling too.

It's close to ten-thirty; there's no time to stop for mail. I drive straight to the *Soon*.

Salakham

At the camp hospital, the pickup is loaded to the tailgate. On the tailgate, in fact, stands Roy Dexter, elevating a fistful of IV bottles connected to sundry of the six patients under the canopy. Under there, too, are an assortment of patients' relatives, and the mother who has a husband in jail, as well as her four-year-old nephew.

It's a happy load. Cruising out of the *Soon*, no questions asked, is inevitably a euphoric experience for those who live behind the guarded gate. Besides, we know we are cutting a rare silhouette with our IV bottles at full mast.

On the edge of town, we turn off the highway and down the cluttered Nongkhai mainstreet that parallels the Mekong. Our passengers eye the storefronts heaped with merchandise. At several intersections I slow down, so they can peer past the palm trees and the river, and see Laos itself. Soon the road widens, with government compounds on both sides. On the right is the Nongkhai Provincial Hospital, a vintage collection of whitewashed buildings set among mature trees. Here we deliver our patients.

The rest of us drive across the road to the *Salakham*, the cluster of buildings housing the provincial government offices. We park by the police headquarters. The place is crowded, inside and out. People eye our strange group—a Lao refugee woman and child, followed by three earnest-looking *falang* (foreigners), Roy, Karen, and myself.

Inside, Roy explains our mission, and there begins a lengthy search of the files for the original complaint. Everyone seems cooperative. But a police station, even in one's own culture, is hardly a pleasant place to sit and wait. In a foreign culture it can be more unsettling; you have so few clues to the secrets in the faces around you.

I recall my first visit here, about a month ago. I was driving out of camp when a policeman flagged me down and asked me to take two passengers into town. I hadn't understood exactly where to take them, but the officer was armed and seemed animated, so I quickly agreed. The passengers turned out to be two frightened-looking Lao country boys who had swum the river the night before and snuck into camp to sleep. And now I, a foreigner, had been deputized to turn the boys in at police headquarters.

The routine on new escapees is that they start with a few days in the local cooler near where they cross the river. Then they are sent to the *Sokoto*, the cramped detention center near the refugee camp, where their case is investigated. This can take weeks or months or longer. When everything checks out, the Thai government accepts them as refugees and transfers them to the refugee camp.

The boys in my car were too scared and tired to talk much. I tried to wish them well, and said I hoped to see

them soon at the camp. We pulled up to the police building, met an officer, and within seconds I saw the boys dis-
appear into the dark building.

Now I sit inside that building and look around. On
each side of the lobby are offices. And then, straight ahead,
I see the bars. The lock-up is poorly lit, but I can count
about twelve people sitting or standing inside. The old lady
next to me nods when I ask if they are from Laos. So this is
the first stop; this was where I had delivered my passengers.

I ponder those faces in the cage. At first they say nothing—no despair, no outrage. Then I imagine I see accep-
tance, a sense that this is a system they understand far better than I, and have calculated the days here and all the
indignities to follow as part of the price for a chance at
building a better life.

The file on our man is located. The police confer briefly
and then tell us that his hearing will come up in July, and
that, pending this, he can be released for the sum of forty
thousand *baht*. We are stunned. That's two thousand dol-
lars. Over the next hour, first here and then at the court-
house next door, we learn that we were wrong in our in-
stant suspicion of blatant Asian graft. This is the local bail
system. We have a choice between posting the full amount,
or buying a bailbond for two thousand *baht*.

Even that is too steep for volunteers like Karen and me.

"I'll pay it," says Roy. "It's for the baby. I do things
like this . . . it's what I'm here for."

But even with the money down, there turns out to be
paper work to do; our man cannot be released until tomorrow. There is no time to argue the point, because it's
now noon and our kids at camp will be waiting for their
ride home to lunch.

(The next afternoon, Roy and I drove the woman and her nephew to the jail for our moment of truth. We waited at the gate for more than an hour. At last her man appeared. And again my Western expectation was confounded: there was almost no outward display of emotion, either here, or later at baby's bedside. The infant was by now desperately ill. He lived two more days. At this writing, there was no word on the father's case.)

Siesta

We hurry back to camp, where the kids are waiting—the last *falang* to leave for lunch. They are all thirsty, because we forgot the thermos this morning.

Also wanting a ride to town is the father of one of the malnourished patients. We say yes, but we always wonder about that. We'll be waved through the gate. But it can be hard for a refugee to finesse his way back into camp. Crazy world!

Today is a scorcher. Fortunately the tropical custom of a midday siesta prevails here. Lunch is from 12 to 2. It's now twelve-thirty. We drop our passenger in town and head south on Friendship Highway the last mile to our place. Our landmark is the stack of teak logs on the side of the road. They are in transit from Laos to Japan. It is the meeting place for neighborhood kids, including our own.

Behind the logs is our Thai bungalow. It has a large room for living, eating, and cooking, and two smaller rooms for sleeping. It is a new masonry house, comfortable, but with nothing done yet to the yard. Our biggest concession to Asian ways is the bathroom. It boasts an Asian squatting toilet in the floor, and a large open cistern in the corner to collect water during the hour or two per day when there is pressure in the mains.

The Asian bath has been perfected over millennia. In the West we have comparable luxuries—bubble baths and pulsating shower heads. But, we seem to have passed up the Asian luxury of slowly ladling tepid cistern water first onto one sweating leg, then another, and a thigh and a chest and a whole exhilarated body. Maybe it missed our culture because the technology is too simple. About all you need is a bathroom with a drain in the floor and a cistern where the water can reach room temperature. The only other equipment is a ladle, which can be half a gourd, or an inexpensive metal bowl engraved with an elaborate Thai design.

An advantage of being the cook in our house is that I get to bathe first. Baths are compulsory here for anyone who has been to camp, especially during a cholera epidemic. Lunch today is easy to make, since the meat and noodles are ready. We have a two-burner camp stove. On one I make a wok of fried noodles, on the other I warm (and sterilize) the French bread in a covered fry pan. And I mix a little batch of hot peppers and Thai fish sauce. That's a new taste for us. But the kids have decided we'll start growing our own hot peppers back in Eden Prairie.

Little Corpse

The afternoon plan is that Karen will work the outpatient clinic, I will meet one of her patients with a resettlement problem, and then teach my English class, Erik and Kris will cover the day care center, and Mali and Mark will stay home this afternoon and do some schoolwork.

As usual, we have stops en route to camp. Karen drops me at the Post and Cable office while she and the kids head to Nongkhai hospital to pick up those X ray patients we delivered this morning.

The IRC post office box yields a nice stack of mail for the expatriates at the camp hospital. It includes two letters for us, and one for us to deliver to a refugee friend named Maha Chanty. I go uptairs to cable Khon Kaen about Karen's arrival.

I am waiting for change, when Kristine comes running up and whispers in my ear. Karen wants me to hurry because we have a corpse in the truck . . . one of the babies we brought in this morning has died.

Out in the parking lot, I see the truck full of patients again, and on one lap there is a little white bundle. Everyone, including our kids, looks sober and controlled. As we drive, Karen explains that it was the baby with suspected cholera and the intestinal obstruction. He had died shortly after admission. The parents wanted to get him back into camp, and Karen had agreed although she doubts the authorities would approve of a cholera corpse being transported through town and into the camp.

We drive into camp without incident, and stop at the hospital. The mother sits in the truck with her bundle, while the father runs in to collect their belongings. They want to be taken to the *Wat* (Buddhist temple) in camp. Karen heads for her box of give-away clothes, and comes out to the mother with a few items for her remaining three children. I see Roy, and ask him to come with us to the *Wat*. Erik and Kris are also along.

The parents sit quietly in back, giving no clues to their feelings. They are both young, and have only recently crossed the river from Laos. They were still in the detention center when their baby got sick, and was transferred to the camp hospital.

The *Wat* is a large tin-roofed shed standing next to the camp market. Both survived the big fire with only a few scorched columns. They are surrounded now by makeshift shelters. As we pull up, I notice that an adult corpse is already laid out on the floor near the entrance to the *Wat*. The mother goes in first. She lays her baby down beside the other corpse. The rest of us follow, bringing their few possessions.

Several bonzes (Buddhist monks) are sitting casually on the platform at the front. They do nothing. Before leaving, I grasp the mother's hand and we share our wet eyes. It is the best I can do from another culture.

From the truck, I watch those bonzes again. Could they be saying more than I think? Could there be some comfort in their attitude? Maybe it says that there's no need here to explain anything . . . you belong . . . bring a corpse if you wish . . . and a tormented mind . . . rest . . . in time we can help you dispose of the body, and the grief. For a society that has traditionally lost half its children before the age of five, there might be caring in what I have seen as callousness.

I can surmise that there will be no cremation for this baby. He will be quietly buried in that section of little mounds on the edge of the camp dump that we call the children's graveyard.

Will we find ways at home of sharing this world? Or must this five-month-long cascade of sorrow and joy be our family secret? We wonder about that. Yes, today tells the story. It belongs in the book.

4

Outpatients

Karen

It's two o'clock and fiercely hot. Dark clouds are forming. We may have a welcome downpour. The benches outside the OPD are crowded with patients, mostly mothers and children. Many I recognize. They have begun keeping follow-up appointments and cultivating some faith in western medicine.

There are two Lao doctors and one medical student seeing outpatients with me today. In the next two hours, I see twenty patietns. They include six children with fevers (two of them with positive malaria smears) . . . three with pneumonia . . . and seven patients with diarrhea, of whom three describe the classic rice water stools of cholera. These we admit with an order for "cholera precautions." One of them defecates on my foot. The public health nurse kindly comes by and douses it with a strong clorox solution.

Here is Thao Eb, an unusual looking 9-month-old boy, much more active now that we have confirmed his thyroid insufficiency and started him on treatment. And we've given him clothes and sent the whole family for feeding supplements. Two of their five children died in Lao hospitals before they escaped. I knew what was going on in their minds when Eb's older sister developed dysentery two weeks ago and had to be hospitalized. She did fine, and was discharged in two days. I will miss seeing Eb when we leave here. Maybe sometime in the States.*

Then comes a little two-year-old with a horrible inflammation of her hand, secondary to some minor injury. We see so many of these. With the redness and swelling spreading up her arm, I decide to admit her for intravenous antibiotics.

I see a boy with clinical hepatitis. I try to explain about fecal contamination. With the open sewers and chronic water shortage here, it's little wonder we see so much infectious hepatitis.

I stop to pour alcohol on my hands. I can't bear to immerse them in the pan with Savlon handwashing liquid. It has flies floating in it. It would take too long to coax someone into changing the solution. So I use alcohol, and my hands are chapped.

It's raining . . . a torrential storm . . . maybe the monsoon season has started. I admit a one-year-old with acute asthma and begin evaluation of a boy with clinical evidence of nephrotic syndrome (a kidney disease).

At four o'clock I run over to make ward rounds again. I make sure the IVs get started on the new suspected cholera patients. The mother of one wipes away stool with her

---

*Eb ended up in Texas, and his sponsor phoned us in Minnesota. We ended up trying to explain in Lao that Eb couldn't go to the clinic today, because it was LBJ's birthday, and the clinic was closed.

Opposite page: Mekong River in dry season.

hand and makes no effort to wash—this less than an hour after I had tried to teach her about fecal hand-mouth contamination. A newly arrived American nurse is visibly annoyed, raising her voice in the hope that comprehension of her English will improve with increasing decibels.

I look around the ward and think.

Of the thirty children here, twenty-eight have diseases that are readily preventable. Only about six or eight kids should be needing hospitalization at any one time in a population of this size . . . that is, if we could do the job that needs doing on nutrition, well-child clinics, immunizations, sanitation, etc. We are moving in that direction, despite obstacles. Preventive programs are the MIHV emphasis. It's what I teach my students. And now it strikes me as ironic that I have worked all of today on acute care—this on the day we have selected to record as a typical one.

Tomorrow, in well-baby clinic, I'll try harder.

5

Potent Dreams Hakon

Erik and Kris took a *samlar* from the *Wat* to the day care center, and I went back to the hospital with Roy. I had mail and money to distribute— matters that should not wait. As usual, there were scores of patients sitting on the benches outside OPD, waiting to be seen by Karen and her colleagues.

The Old Man

I decided there would be time to make a personal delivery of the letter to Maha Chanty. I headed for his shack at the other end of the camp.

Maha Chanty is a venerable Lao teacher from Luang Prabang, the Royal Capital of Laos. We had known him there in the sixties. Recently, at age 77, he had escaped from Laos with his family. The letter we had was from Jim De Cou, a former foreign service colleague, who has been arranging a sponsor for the family in the Washington, DC area.

I should have walked to Chanty's place, or gone by *samlar.* Driving through camp is the slowest way to go. The dirt roadways are nearly always crammed with people and water carts and *samlars.* I parked a few hundred yards from Chanty's place. It was easier to jump the stream of open sewage, than to try fording it and risk getting stuck. The family saw me coming, and by the time I reached the shack, the patriarch was getting up from his siesta.

Chanty, his wife, daughter, son-in-law, and two small children lived in an area about ten feet wide and sixteen feet deep. It was a segment of a masonry building with a tin roof that contained about thirty similar units.

Chanty had moved here after the big fire, which destroyed his earlier cubicle—of about the same size, but constructed of thatch and bamboo with a tin roof. Two months later most of the 20,000 homeless were still living in temporary shacks and tents. Chanty was among the lucky ones who had moved into one of the empty units in the Hmong section of the camp. They had been vacated late last year when the Hmong refugees (the largest mountain-tribe in Laos) were moved to the camp at Ban Vinai.

But today Chanty had a new problem. The tin roof on his side of the building had blown off a few days ago in the pre-monsoon rains. He and his neighbors now had a sagging tarp for a roof, courtesy of one of the relief agencies. The flapping above us warned that a storm was again brewing.

The Chanty home had three sections. A small strip of dirt floor inside the door contained a charcoal cooking stove, water pots, etc. Here stood Chanty's wife. Next was a central raised section with straw mats on it. Here the son-in-law was weaving a rice basket and his wife feeding the baby. In the back was a curtain with sleeping mats behind it.

The household greeted their visitor with usual Lao graciousness. They were delighted with Jim's letter, and the enclosed snapshot of Chanty from the sixties. He was then the leading commentator on Radio Luang Prabang. The letter asked how the family's resettlement processing was coming along, and we reviewed that.

Chanty had crossed the river last November. By December he had moved into camp, unofficially, while still on the roster at the detention center. This was a common practice among refugees who could afford some modest bribes. During this hiatus, the family received neither housing nor food in the camp, nor could they register for resettlement to a third country. In January, Chanty's family was accepted as refugees by the Thai Government. Through the camp grapevine he knew when to reappear at the detention center to answer the roll-call of those officially released to the refugee camp. The family now got quarters and a rice ration in camp. And now they could register for resettlement to the United States.

Shortly after registering, the entire family was summoned to a pre-screening interview with an American. There followed months of uncertainty while the information taken at the pre-screening was checked and processed. Finally, last week, Chanty had been called back for his second interview. Here his case was given a final check before going to the INS (Immigration and Naturalization Service). All had gone well, and Chanty was now scheduled for an INS interview next week. Barring an unexpected hitch, he would then get his "T-number"—a wildly significant bureaucratic form letter, bearing a number starting with "T," authorizing transit to the United States.

There would still follow several more months of waiting, while his file filtered down through the resettlement agencies to a specific sponsor in the United States—in this case a group of churches with whom Jim was working.

Despite our perception that Chanty's case was dragging interminably, it was going better than most. It seemed likely, in fact, that he would leave camp within six months of arrival*, which is presently the minimum waiting period for refugees resettling to the U.S. For others, the uncertainty can drag on for a year, or for years.

As we chatted in the hot afternoon, the storm released its load. My hosts knew exactly where to place the pots and basins to catch the leaks from the tarp.

I reminded Chanty that his baby grandson would soon be growing up in a typical American community, with no comprehension of his roots here, or in Laos. This child and his peers would one day cherish their snatches of understanding of this period. They would hope that there had been a literate man then, who had preserved an account of the deterioration in Laos, of the flight across the Mekong, of the long hard wait in a refugee camp—and then the encounter with a new life. I suggested that Maha Chanty was better equipped for that task than any Lao I knew. The old man glowed with purpose, and promised to try.

The Peasant

From Chanty's place, I headed back to the hospital to meet the father of a child with measles-encephalitis. Karen had gathered that he had some overwhelming problem about his resettlement, and I had agreed to go with him at three to the interview center.

---

*It actually took fourteen months. Maha Chanty and his family arrived in Maryland in February 1981.

He told me he and his family had been in the camp for a year. He didn't seem to know whether or not he was registered for resettlement, or where he stood in the process of getting out. But he wanted to go to America!

Although the steps in the resettlement sequence was a dominant topic of discussion in the camp, there still seemed to be an inordinate number of people who failed to comprehend the system, or who feigned ignorance when there was a chance that a *falang* might carry their ball.

This case might be of the latter variety. Yet, who was I to belittle the ego strength it must take for a traditional Lao peasant to assert himself in the neat western channels of our resettlement process. The real marvel is surely that so many of them do learn to work our system.

We took the short walk to the interview center and met one of the refugees who works there as a translator. I asked the father to explain his problem in Lao. The answers we got were polite, but only generalities. It took Western assertiveness to get to the bottom of this man's problem: Yes, he had registered with the Americans, but he had failed to appear for his pre-screening interview, because his boy was sick. . . . No, he could not reschedule the interview until his whole family could appear with him. . . . But, YES, as soon as his boy got better, he could come in and reschedule the interview. His face radiated an enormous relief.

I wondered how many similar bundles of fear and uncertainty were wandering around this camp. Shouldn't this place have a full-time cross-cultural *ombudsman*?

The Nurses

It was three-thirty, time for the English and orientation class for Lao nurses at the hospital. We met daily in the "injection room" of the OPD. I have a similar class for Lao doctors three days a week at eleven.

By three-forty-five, the injections were long finished, and students were just beginning to wander in. This was three-thirty "Lao time," and we had talked about that. They knew that before long they would have to start living by Western time. And we laughed.

We had no curriculum or teaching materials. Our goals were to learn spoken English, and to learn about living in Western countries. Our program was to pick a topic and talk about it in English until we had enough to write a drill on the blackboard. Then we would practice the drill and memorize it.

In recent lessons we had practiced going to restaurants. Last time, we went to lunch, and before that we had breakfast. Today, it would be dinner on the town. We could go to McDonalds, or to the Holiday Inn. We wrote some typical menu items on the board. And we talked about the cost of our evening for a family living on one or two minimum wages.

"What'll ya have?"

"Pepsi, hamburger, french fry," said Ponsi, the careful one.

We worked on that, even noting that the American custom of ordering food and drink—in that order—had as little logic as the opposite order.

"One beer, one cheeseburger," said Souba, the extrovert.

"We don't sell beer at McDonalds. Try the Holiday Inn."

His bride, Dongmali, went straight to the Holiday Inn—and ignored their menu.

"Omelette! Champagne!" she blurted.

But most of the class had been sobered by our cost analysis. Plain hamburgers were the solid favorite.

The rationale for English and orientation classes at the hospital is a simple matter of reciprocity. Westerners have descended on the camp hospital obsessed with improving the quality of health care, and discover a Lao medical staff whose obsession, not at all surprisingly, is a continent away. So we share our obsessions, and everybody wins.

It was close to five when the class ended. Karen was winding up on the ward, and Erik and Kris were back from day care. The *falang* had gathered around the vehicles outside the hospital, making small-talk. Karen was still delayed, so at five-fifteen we went to our usual tactic of loading up and starting the engine. They let her go. And tonight, she informed me, I would not get the first shower. A kid with cholera had defecated on her foot!

6

Teens & Pre-teens Erik

Dad suggests we record feelings, as much as events. Here goes.

Waking up is a chore. Mom usually gets up first. I sleep on the roll-away in the living room, so she comes right by me to unbolt the door to go out jogging. Once I'm awake, I usually join her. And I enjoy it. But sometimes, like this morning, I don't want to get up yet, and I feign sleep.

When she comes back in, she asks me to turn on VOA (the Voice of America on short-wave radio), and then I have to get up because I'm the only one who can fine-tune it. I've become a short-wave buff. That's something we never knew about at home. Most countries broadcast in English, and they all have their own style. The same piece of news sounds different in every country. You get to where you can identify them in a few seconds.

A morning at home is more peaceful than at the *Soon*. But the job I had today was close to impossible. I was trying to copy information from 1979 hospital charts written in a cross between Lao, French and English. I read only English. Sometimes we didn't know what language the stuff was in; Mom and Dad couldn't read them either. I don't think we'll learn much from this study, like we did on the nutrition survey. On that one, we weighed and measured three hundred kids, and then all the tabulating paid off. We had hard data on malnutrition where most people had assumed that there was no problem at our camp.

I'm on "pick-up" this week, which means I had to straighten up a bit before the others came home for lunch. The kids rotate four sets of jobs on a weekly basis. The hardest of them is dishes, and Kris is on that this week. Dad sterilizes them after we wash them. The question today was whether Kris had to do lunch dishes until Dad had sterilized breakfast dishes. She won. Mali's job this week is sweeping the house and washing down the patio, and Mark is on dusting, which is everybody's favorite week, because it's the easiest to fake. These jobs aren't hard, and we had the same sort of thing at home. But getting them done can easily be the biggest hassle of the day.

I did no homework today. All of us have more or less finished the work we had along from school. Mali has some math left—that's definitely not her subject. And I have a chapter to go in Spanish. How can I get into Spanish in Thailand? The first few months here, we had to work every day on schoolwork. I'm in ninth grade, Kris in seventh, Mali in sixth, and Mark is in the fifth grade. Our schools at home gave us work to take along so we don't expect to lose any grades.

Lunch was a bit rushed today. It's usually a nice time. You get to clean up, drink as much water as you want, and eat. After lunch there's usually time for a short nap. But not today.

The afternoon ride to the *Soon* was sobering. But I didn't really think all that much about it being a dead body. I was more worried about spreading cholera. I think Mom was too.

The back of the pickup is a special place. Usually we kids ride alone there. It is a hidden vantage point from which I can see all that goes on as we drive by. But the Thai kids can't see me and yell "falang, falang."

The *samlar* drivers are all different. The one today was nice. You get a good feeling about one like that. With others you can't wait to get off. With some you can pay the Lao rate of one *baht* (5 cents) to anywhere in camp, but I usually feel guilty and end up paying the *falang* rate of two *baht*.

The day care center is in a building that used to be another hospital (when the Hmong were here). It's used now for public health clinics, and for a dental clinic. Until a few weeks ago, we always came up here with the Taylors. They worked in the dental clinic; he's a retired dental surgeon who was here with IRC. The Lao and the *falang* all liked the Taylors. This place seems empty since they went home.

To get to day care, you walk past the crush of people waiting for shots or something. They stare, and I feel self-conscious. It's a relief to be inside. I feel at home playing with the little kids, and watching the Lao mothers teach the traditional dances. The self-concious feeling peaks about once a week, when I go over to CRS (Catholic Relief Services) two blocks away to get more high-protein biscuits. Walking back is an awful experience. You have two big boxes of food, while the staring refugees have almost nothing.

Kristine spends more time than any of us in the day care center. She is considered the manager of the center. She writes:

Mali and I took a *samlar* from the hospital across the camp to day care. We met the two Lao mothers, Phensy and Somnuck, who work at the center. Phensy's six-year-old daughter, Ja-a, and Somnuck's four-year-old brother, Youk, were also there.

Day care meets in a large room, about twenty by forty feet, that used to be a hospital ward. We have morning and afternoon sessions, each with about thirty kids, who are with us for two months. They are supposed to be between three and five years old, but most of them are much older than they look, so we have lots of six, seven, and eight year olds too. Our purposes are to give parents a break, to give the kids a good meal, and to introduce them to things like washing hands, brushing teeth, saying the ABCs, and feeling comfortable around *falang* like us.

After we had set out the toys, Phensy went to the door to call the roll of the children. We lined up for exercises, which included jumping jacks and jogging around the room. Then we let the kids play for a half hour, and we and the mothers kidded around together with snatches of our Lao and their English. After that Mali and I took turns drilling the kids on their ABCs and the mothers taught them some Lao songs and they did the Lao dance called the *Lamvong*. It is very graceful. Then the kids played some more and tried to get piggy-back rides from us. We also went through the tooth-brushing exercise and played some American games, including London Bridge.

At eleven, everybody washed hands and we

served a lunch of rice with a vegetable and meat topping, and clean water. The meal was cooked by the Food for the Hungry station next door. We got the kids ready to go home, and as each one left we taught them to say "good-bye sister." Then we took a *samlar* back to the hospital.

Mali was at day care this morning and at home this afternoon. She assures us that she did some math. She writes:

While we waited for Mom at noon, Kris helped with the feeding on the ward, and I helped in the pharmacy, counting out pills for prescriptions. Then we went home.

No kidding, I did do several pages of math, but I hate dividing decimals! Later, I heard some of the kids outside. It was Noei, Oie, and Phon and a bunch of the other neighbor kids. They pointed to our bicycles. Mark and I locked up the house and got on our bikes. We rode down to the *wat* and back, with them jabbering away in Thai. I understood only a few words.

Noei pointed to the teak logs and said, "Bai lin yoo poon" (go play over there). So we dropped our bikes under the mango tree and started climbing the logs. First we played hide-and-go-seek in Thai, and then Mark went in the house to get his soccer ball, and we kicked that around. Before long the yellow pick-up truck turned in our driveway, and the afternoon had ended much too soon.

Mark worked this morning and played this afternoon, except for all the time he spent dusting. He writes:

I worked with Toshiko, the Japanese lady at

Food for the Hungry. First I washed cups. Then I went on errands with Toshiko. She had a folder with the names of kids we were looking for. We went to the house of one kid, but when we got there it was not the one we were looking for. But she gave him a card for getting food anyway.

Then I took a *samlar* back to the hospital. A *samlar* is a three-wheeled cart that you ride like a tricycle. It has a place in back for people to sit on, or to carry things. At the hospital I helped Debbie file the cards in the OPD. Then it was lunch time, but we had to wait for Mom and Dad.

The things that I like about the camp are that there are a lot of nice people, and many things to do.

In the evening, we all took showers, and Dad got supper ready. It was good. We think we'll eat a lot more rice when we get back to the States.

Then Mom and Dad had to make a phone call to Bangkok about a new nurse who's coming. A phone call here is a big operation. You drive down to the phone company, place your call, and pray you don't have to wait too long.

They were back in an hour. We were relaxing, but they each had one more project in them.

Mom got most of us to join her for the nightly sessions with the Thai language tapes. (Thai and Lao are related, about like the Scandinavian languages.)

And Dad wanted everyone to start writing up our typical day.

Eventually, he got something.

PART TWO

The Refugees

7
Profile

Nineteen-eighty is only an average year for refugees. We have about ten million of them around the world. In 1971, we had that number among the Bengalis alone. And after World War II, we had probably twenty million or more refugees.[1]

From 1975 to 1980, more than one million refugees fled the communist countries of Southeast Asia—by boat, by land, and by swimming the Mekong river.

In those five years, more than 485,000 refugees from Laos, Cambodia, and Vietnam sought asylum in Thailand.[2] Of these, about 194,000 had been resettled in third countries, some 59% of them in the United States.

That left about 280,000 refugees in Thailand, plus an

---

[1]From a lecture by Louis Wiesner, Counselor, International Rescue Committee, at International Health Course, University of Minnesota Medical School, Nov. 1979.

[2]From an April 30, 1980, summary by the American embassy in Bangkok.

additional 400,000 Khmer (Cambodians) who were not formally classified as refugees.

At Nongkhai, in early 1980, Lao refugees were coming in at about a thousand a month, and in May (our last month there) it was four thousand.

The overwhelming needs of many of these people—and the willingness of a small country like Thailand to keep its borders open to such an influx—has spurred international and voluntary efforts to help the refugees in the camps, and to help them start new lives in other countries. MIHV is a tiny example of such efforts.

Survivors

But the picture we get of refugees as a helpless mass of pitiful humanity can be quite misleading. There is much more than that to the refugees.

Most of them are refugees by choice. They have deliberately chosen to flee rather than submit to some unacceptable affront. In the case of the Hmong tribe—under systematic annihilation by the Communists in Laos—it isn't much of a choice. In the case of the lowland Lao, there are more options.

Of those who make the choice to flee, only a fraction arrive in a refugee camp. Some will have their plans discovered. Some will be caught as they leave. Some will die en route of disease or hunger, especially among the Hmong, where the secret flight through mountain jungles can take months. Some will drown in the Mekong, from exhaustion or bullet wounds. Some will find the boat they hired was run by bandits or Communist agents. Some will be raped on arrival. Some will make it, weakened, to the detention center only to die there from the overwhelming exposure to infectious disease.

A fresh volunteer, standing in the hospital ward of a refugee camp, may at first see only helpless, pitiful people. With time, he learns that he is in the presence of one of the most rigorously selected populations on earth. It is first self-selected. It is then further selected by a ruthless environment. The survivors of this process tend to be an incredibly resourceful group of human beings.

Volunteers at Nongkhai could only stand in awe at the reaction of the refugees on the night of February 15, 1980, when a fire swept through the camp in forty-five minutes, leveling the straw and bamboo homes of 20,000 people. By our standards, such a tragedy should have yielded a high incidence of injury, shock, and general inability to cope. Here there was one death, a few hundred minor burns, and one case of hyperventilation attributed to stress. There was almost no panic or looting. By next morning, the refugees were bending gracefully over the warm ashes, scraping for valuables and for bits of wire and nails to use in improvising new shelters.

In part, this response could be attributed to the Lao culture—the Asian admiration for the bamboo stalk that bends with the wind. Primarily, though, it was an expression of the pervasive coping ability of refugees.

The refugees don't flaunt these qualities. They seem delighted, when there is an opportunity, to luxuriate in a dependency role. They face the same culture gap that we do. They, too, can see themselves as pitiful and helpless in comparison to the rich, omnipotent Westerners.

But, behind those wretched facades are the real refugees, and they tend to be splendid human beings.

The Gleam

At Nongkhai the air is alive with a sense of change.

Few of these refugees expect to spend the rest of their lives in the camp. And, whatever the change brings, it is almost certain to be better than the present. So they tend to be basically optimistic about the future. Despite their appalling circumstances, they seem to have a gleam in their eyes. This can have a powerful effect on people around them (and be a hard thing for volunteers to explain back home).

Refugees, worldwide, have been described as a self-selection of the most venturesome, rebellious, energetic, aggressive, and sometimes quarrelsome members of their societies. Some of them had no choice but to flee. Those who were the elite in their former societies might have exaggerated expectations in their new world. But the majority are surprisingly adaptable, work hard at jobs that no one else will take, and rise rapidly.[3]

Throughout history, refugees have suffered, and some have survived. They always looked pitiful and helpless. No one expected much from them. But they had the gleam in their eyes. And they invigorated every society they touched. For the Statue of Liberty, Emma Lazarus wrote:

> Give me your tired, your poor,
> Your huddled masses yearning to breathe free,
> The wretched refuse of your teeming shore.
> Send these, the homeless, tempest-tossed to me.
> I lift my lamp beside the golden door!

---

[3]Weisner.

8

Escape to Thailand

In Laos, when somebody vanishes, it's best not to ask where they went. There are usually two possibilities. They have gone to the "seminar" for re-education. Or they have escaped to Thailand.

There is no more unlikely place on earth for such a state of affairs than the peaceful, friendly Kingdom of Laos—the Land of a Million Elephants and White Parasol, as it was officially called until 1975. Then it became a People's Democratic Republic, under Vietnamese domination.

There began an exodus from Laos, and it never stopped. Five years later it yields an average of four thousand refugees every month—about a quarter of a million people since 1975. Laos had a population of about three million.

Who are these refugees?

The Hmong

One segment is the Hmong tribe. The Lao and the

Hmong live near each other, but at different altitudes—the Lao in the valley, and the Hmong on the mountain. The Lao exist casually as extended families. The Hmong are clans in an organized tribe. They are nomadic, independent, and share the Western tendency to polarize on issues. In the decade when the United States needed every friend it had in Southeast Asia, the Hmong were our most understanding allies, and fierce fighters of the communists. (The Lao were also our friends, but they found anti-communism almost as preposterous as communism.)

The Hmong are still fighting, more for their lives now than for the liberation of Laos. Those that get out describe a holocaust, an attempt to eliminate the tribe in Laos. Probably less than half of those who start their escape make it as far as the refugee camp.

At nine one morning, a sixty-year-old man in a coma arrived in our emergency room. He was carried by two confused and exhausted-looking Hmong teenagers. During the night, the man, his wife, and two boys had culminated their two-month hike out of Laos. The mother was shot and killed in the river. The others made it. We suspected the father had malaria. We tried all the heroics we had; he didn't respond. The boys stood by all day as their father slipped away. At one point we sent them out for some noodles; they hadn't eaten in days. The next morning they came with a pathetic delegation from the decimated group that had crossed together. They took the old man's body out.

What would happen to those boys? They would be sent to the Hmong camp at Ban Vinai. And some time hence they would probably end up in an American community, quiet newcomers, unlikely to give much hint of their rending initiation into manhood.

The Lao

Among the ethnic Lao, the exodus began with the departure of the old elite—the former government, military and business leaders. But soon the mix of refugees had reached deep into the population at large, and included peasant families from the villages as well as townspeople.

The miracle baby is in the camp. At age four months he left Laos with his father, mother, uncle, aunt and two cousins. They planned to swim. His father carried him. His mother was a poor swimmer, and half way across she drowned. The father, in an effort to save her, tossed the baby to his uncle. Then the shooting began, killing the aunt and the cousins. Almost to the Thai shore, a bullet hit the uncle, who then threw the baby toward land. Thai villagers saw it, and ran to get the baby. The father made it too. We treated the miracle baby for malaria, from which he also recovered.

Fortunately, attrition rates on crossing the Mekong were not usually that high. But the odds were still grim. It was rare in camp to meet a family that was not missing someone, either from the crossing or from the terror that drove them to escape.

They described a tyranny in Laos that was both political and caloric—"We couldn't live under communism," and "We couldn't get enough to eat." The Lao would not usually volunteer their story to a Westerner. But behind those quiet faces waiting outside the clinic could lie harrowing tales—if you asked, and understood a little of their language.

Some had a price on their heads from their association with the former government. Some had escaped from "the seminar." One man cried as he told of having to dig a hole as deep as he was tall, being forced to stand in it, and having his head kicked by the communist soldiers. He had severe neurologic consequences. One doctor friend said he failed in several attempts to escape his re-education camp, and finally allowed himself to become very sick. Eventually, he was sent to Vientiane for treatment, and then slipped across the river.

Many told of severe food shortages, especially in Vientiane and the larger towns—a preposterous predicament for a lush, underpopulated paradise like Laos.

Those were factors that drove people from Laos. There were also positive factors that attracted them to camp.

The prospect of starting a new life in a new society appealed to resourceful people such as refugees. Many wanted to join relatives who were already in new countries. Even the limited food and shelter in the refugee camp was an attraction. But at the price of the crossing, it was no route to a free lunch.

Looking Back

"We told no one," said those who made it over. A Lao doctor confided, "My father still doesn't know where I am. My sister knows, but she tells him I'm very busy at the hospital. It's better. If he knows something, they might accuse him."

Laos is six hundred miles long. Along its entire underside it shares a winding border with Thailand, first through mountains and then down the long Mekong River. It is a border that can extract a human toll from those who cross it, but it can not be sealed. From Chiang Rai in the north, to Ubon in the south, there were eight refugee camps along the Thai frontier, receiving a steady traffic of new arrivals.

Despite the blood in the Mekong, and the political differences between its banks, there were many bonds between the Thai and the Lao. They are of the same ethnic stock, and have close similarities in language, culture, and expectation of life. Diplomatic and commercial relations remained intact.

At Nongkhai, the ferry still ran for those with papers in order—businessmen, officials, and Russian shoppers in Nongkhai's loaded storefronts.

We were also aware of some Lao who crossed with government permission to use our medical facilities. One was a four-year-old boy, bitten by a rabid dog, confirmed by the Lao laboratory in Vientiane. There was no rabies vaccine in Laos, so they sent him to us. We got him vaccine, but we had no hyper immune globulin. We feared for his life. Others came with requests for routine antibiotics. They couldn't all have been spies; the Thai were quite efficient in weeding them out.

There were also clandestine links. These seemed to exist, not so much for insurgency purposes, as to enable poor refugees to send food and clothing to their even poorer relatives in Laos. Everything seemed to be in short supply there.

Some refugees saw the signs of paralysis across the river as confirming their faith that change was coming in Laos. There was a new revolution brewing, they said. And some were undoubtedly involved in its plans. The problem with such dreams would not be the Lao brothers across the river. It would be their Vietnamese masters.

The Hmong were especially reluctant to abandon the dream of liberating their homeland. At Ban Vinai there were still many "no-shows" at the moment of truth when they had to board the buses for resettlement overseas.

Among the Lao, though, most of the country's best nationalists were boarding the buses every month, ready to give their energy to some other society. Even Doctor Bounthene, the dedicated chief of the Lao physicians in camp hospital for the last five years, decided, for the sake of her three children and her husband, to apply for resettlement with their relatives in North Carolina.

It was sad to see a country lose its most vigorous people. But who had the courage to ask them to stay?

It was hard to imagine a worse mismatch between a national character and a style of government than that which existed in Laos. The only comfort lay in the thought that, if anyone could beguile a dictatorship into impotence, it would surely be the Lao.

9

The Sokoto

A new escapee from Laos is not yet a refugee. First he must spend weeks and maybe months in the Sokoto, the detention center where new arrivals are cleared for admission to Thailand as refugees.

The Sokoto looks like a run-down cavalry fort in a grade B cowboy movie. High walls of wood and corrugated roofing enclose an area of about one acre, where up to four thousand people live in makeshift shacks. The population fluctuates widely, but when it is crowded there is not enough room for everyone to lie down at the same time. There is filth everywhere. At the gate are peep-holes, crammed with faces looking out on the dream of a better future.

Inmates receive a daily ration of food. But it is rarely enough. There is also a restaurant in the Sokoto for those with some money.

The population of the Sokoto is about half Hmong and half Lao. The Hmong will eventually be transferred to the Hmong camp at Ban Vinai, about a five-hour drive to the west. The Lao will come a half mile down the road to the Lao refugee camp.

The most practical course for the Lao, if they can afford the small bribes involved, is to buy their way out of the Sokoto and back in again, as Maha Chanty did.

For the Hmong, this course is much harder to arrange, because their camp is far away and they do not blend into the Thai population, as the Lao do. The Hmong usually have the longest stay at the Sokoto.

Not surprisingly, the Sokoto is a constant breeding ground of infectious diseases. There is a simple ten-bed medical unit in the Sokoto, operated by CRS (Catholic Relief Services). But those who are very sick, of both Lao and Hmong, are sent over to the Lao refugee hospital, where they are often the most critical cases on our wards.

CRS has opened a tent city at the south end of the refugee camp to accommodate the overflow from the Sokoto. They are working with the Thai authorities to expand the tent city so the Sokoto can be closed down.

Mouth to Mouth

Vichit, the IRC Thai coordinator, talked with the guard through a peep-hole. The gate opened for us, and was locked behind us.

We were at the Sokoto with three deans from the medical school at Khon Kaen University, whom we had invited to visit the refugee medical program at Nongkhai.

Today, the Sokoto was relatively uncrowded; you could pick your way forward between the clusters of staring humanity. We came to the pavilion that housed the medical unit. The Lao medic ran up to us. A baby was having seizures and had stopped breathing.

Opposite page:
Above: Samlars and water carts
Below: Camp hospital after fire.

Karen and the three deans rushed to the matside. Adrenalin? No, there was none. An airway? None here. Karen bent over the baby in mouth-to-mouth resuscitation. He's breathing! IV fluid? Yes, we have some.

For twenty minutes the foursome struggled to start an IV with an oversized needle. It was an unusual emergency team—a biochemist, a pathologist, an internist, and Karen the pediatrician.

Let's take him to the camp hospital, said Karen. With the baby still convulsing, we rushed to the gate (which mysteriously opened) and screeched over to the camp.

At the camp hospital, a Lao New Year's party was in progress. But the revelers saw us coming. The key people rushed to the emergency room. Within minutes the child was stable. Later that afternoon, Roy confirmed in the lab that the child had meningitis.

The mouth-to-mouth resuscitator went on antibiotics. The deans reflected on the searing realism of their tour to the refugee camp. And all of us, at some level of our awareness, pondered that law of coincidences which had enabled an infant in the Sokoto to attracts a team of four physicians to his miserable mat at precisely the moment when he needed them.

10

Life at the Soon

The 30 to 40 thousand residents of the Lao refugee camp at Nongkhai, Thailand, make it the second largest Lao community anywhere—after Vientiane, the capital of Laos, sitting across the river, a few miles upstream.

The camp was opened in 1975. It has been considered one of the more stable of the refugee camps along the borders of Thailand. During the first five months of 1980, it took in about 10,000 new refugees, while about 7,000 left for resettlement in other countries.

Almost all the refugees in the Nongkhai camp are ethnic Lao, but there are small minorities of Chinese-Lao, Vietnamese-Lao, and tribal groups such as the Black Thai.

The refugee camp is a small city—Lao style—with a market, and hundreds of tiny thatch-hut enterprises offering everything from herbal medicine to a sometimes-functioning xerox machine. The place buzzes a bit more than one might expect in a Lao town, perhaps because refugees tend to be the more vigorous members of their society. But it is still the quintessence of a Lao community, with all the incongruities a Westerner would expect to encounter, including even the muddled remains of our successive attempts to be helpful.

Hunger

Despite all the Lao enterprise, and all the international programs, a lot of people cannot get enough to eat here. Of all the health hazards the refugees face—malaria, dysenteries, TB, measles—the biggest one by far is malnutrition. Life in the camp revolves around the battle against hunger.

For many refugees the problem begins before they arrive in camp. Some are hungry in Laos, and some lose ground, nutritionally, in the escape. Then they land in the Sokoto, and lose more ground.

Once they are legally registered in the camp, refugees are eligible for a basic food allotment, financed through the UN High Commission for Refugees (UNHCR). It consists primarily of rice—about fifteen kilos per month per person. There are also small amounts of fish, meat, vegetables, sauces, hot peppers, and salt. The allotment is distributed about twice a month.

Many people question the equity of this distribution. Many others wonder if they could do much better, given the realities of international bungling, Asian graft, and the Lao tendency to group as extended families. The consensus seems to be that most refugees, most of the time, can expect to receive some of their food allotment. But no one can expect to live adequately on their allotment alone. And there will always be some who miss out on all or most of it.

The central fact of life at the Soon is that all the refugees need to supplement their food allotment. Some, but not all, are able to do so.

Enterprise

A minority of perhaps ten percent of the refugees are, by Lao standards, relatively affluent, either from outside wealth, or from successful enterprises in camp. Some of these are important spenders in the shops and movie houses of Nongkhai itself.

Others have relatives already resettled abroad, who can send them a small check from time to time. About a quarter of the families seem to have some such arrangement.

Most refugees find ways to earn a little money in camp.

Strong young men with some capital can buy a *samlar* for about 3,000 *baht* ($150), and if they have the energy to pedal hard, they can gross up to 100 *baht* a day ($5). Softer work pays much less. The hundreds of stalls and vending carts selling drinks or a few staples can be tended all day for a few *baht* of profit. Nurses at the camp hospital earn a stipend of 400 *baht* a month. Lao doctors get 800 *baht*. Some doctors and nurses set up thatch-hut "clinics," where injections (a favorite Lao treatment) sell for 20 *baht* apiece. A few even do abortions, and the hospital treats the resulting septicemia in women.

Handicrafts abound—weaving, embroidery, basketry, carpentry—either for use in the local life style, or as souvenirs for expatriates. The camp even boasts a furniture "factory" that sells its rattan bookshelves in town and beyond.

There are restaurants and newsstands and barber shops and beauty parlors and tailor shops, crammed into extensions of people's quarters, or tucked into shacks along the main walkways. There are many signs for photographers and resume writers—important enterprises in a place where everyone is preparing applications for resettlement.

And there are hundreds of water carts—fifty-gallon drums on wheels, gaily painted, selling water door-to-door. Standing in line for water can consume much of a refugee's day. The water carts are a boon to those who can afford to buy, and to those who need a job. There are even a few private wells, sunk by enterprising refugees, where you pay for your water, but the line is shorter. Nevertheless, water remains in chronic short supply. An average family can spend six baht a day for minimum water needs, and it is not uncommon to hear that a family spends half its income on water.

A few refugees get permission to work in town, mostly as low-paid household help, but some in professional positions. The higher the pay, though, the more pay-offs will be needed. We know an engineer who declined a top job in town because it was cheaper to stay home babysitting while his wife worked as a nurse. But the Nongkhai tennis courts boast two refugee pros—a reminder that, in the good old days, the Lao elite often excelled on the courts.

From this barrage of enterprise, a tiny segment of refugees become comfortably affluent. But the vast majority of them earn barely enough to maintain a minimum diet. And some can't make it. Free feeding stations—operated by Food for the Hungry, Catholic Relief Services and several church groups—try to help the obviously malnourished ones or those not yet getting rations.

But every day, in the hospital clinic, we treat malnourished children, typically from large families with only one parent left to cope. And every day, in cooperation with the feeding stations, we write out regular prescriptions for the most potent medicine in camp—food.

Housing

Housing for refugees at the Nongkhai camp is a confused mixture of barracks, shacks, and tents—a variety stemming mainly from the fire that leveled most of the tight rows of tin-roofed pavilions, and forced people to improvise new shelters.

The barracks are long open structures, divided into a series of open bays on each side, measuring about ten feet wide and twenty feet deep. Each houses an extended family. Some are masonry structures, but most are temporary, made of bamboo, tin and PVC, that were rushed to completion after the fire.

But the dominant structures of the campscape are shacks, huts, and lean-to's, mostly assembled from the charred scraps of the burned buildings. They are generally smaller than the barracks bays, but many refugees prefer them for their greater privacy. (Suburbia again?) Most of them are builder-occupied, but a few are rental properties. The units are bought and sold between arriving and departing refugees.

Another dominant architectural form is the tiny bath house—scores of them, each about three feet square, scattered all over camp. The Lao love to bathe. They are accustomed to an open country, with always a river nearby, and in the hot dry season they go to it often for a cooling bath. The camp is crowded, and it has no river. But the most impoverished Lao will find a way to pour water over his body in the Asian fashion. The bath stalls are usually made from bits of charred tin roofing from the fire. Here the refugee can retreat with his pail of expensive water—and restore both body and soul. Those who can afford neither water nor a bath house will come with rope and bucket to the burned-out area of the camp and find an abandoned surface well with a little water in it. Here, behind their loose sarongs, they bathe gracefully in public, and wave happily to passers-by.

All this cleanliness has an irony, at least for the Western mentality. The same Lao who practice an impeccable personal hygiene, seem to be remarkly tolerant of their unsanitary surroundings. Most public toilets in camp are plugged. Open sewers often overflow from neglect. And garbage removal never seems to work right. To get together on something like keeping a public sewer open seems to be more complicated, to the Lao mentality, than finding clean ways to walk around the mess. (The Hmong, in contrast, can go months without a bath, but would easily organize a daily garbage detail. They, of course, have lived high above the river culture. But their tribal orientation makes it easier for them to address group concerns.)

Organization

But, the camp administration at Nongkhai is itself so unworkable as to absolve everybody from much responsibility for all the things that don't go right.

There are three separate hierarchies of responsibility.

Control of all activities rests ultimately with the Royal Thai Government, which operates the camps through the Ministry of the Interior, with input from other Ministries such as Health and Defense. But Thailand has asked the rest of the world to help carry some of the load of keeping its borders open to refugees. This is done primarily through the UN High Commission for Refugees. The UNHCR budget for refugee programs in Thailand in 1980 is $107,000,000. The UNHCR also tries to coordinate the vast array of foreign voluntary agencies (VOLAGS) that have come to help the refugees.

In addition, each camp has a refugee hierarchy of its own, which has little direct authority, but considerable influence over the "end use" of whatever supplies and decisions filter down. At Nongkhai there is a Lao Committee, with a chairman and chiefs for each building, who see to the final allocation of food and housing (and to organizing the garbage details).

The three hierarchies—the Thai, the internationals, and the Lao—have many common objectives in Nongkhai. But each has its own strengths and weaknesses, and each has some agenda items the others do not have. None of the three seems particularly sensitive to what the others are about. Here are Karen's notes from the first VOLAG coordinating committee she attended at Nongkhai, chaired by the UNHCR.

Meeting set for ten a.m., began at eleven, and lasted until two. Minutes of previous meeting dealt with toilet construction and pumping, camp security, need for fire trucks and a sprinkler system (three weeks later, camp burned down), garbage disposal, need for more expatriate health care providers, and need to close illegal pharmacies in camp. There was lengthy discussion of new plan to tighten security at main gate (plan lasted one week). At end of discussion someone noted that large segments of camp fence were missing and ought to be repaired. Lao commander was asked to arrange to keep water tanks around camp filled from wells and towers. He requested a hundred trucks to do the job. There was inconclusive discussion of fact that half the toilets in camp were currently overflowing, that the original contract for toilet pumping was inadequate, and that not all toilets could be pumped. There followed discussion of need for garbage removal and general clean-up. It was felt refugees should be penalized for not cleaning up themselves, but no consensus on what penalty to impose. Lao commander suggested they needed better tools, and that existing garbage cans were too heavy. Representative of Norwegian Church Relief bemoaned lack of competition among VOLAGS for the garbage business, and volunteered to provide more tools. Under health matters, IRC medical director reported that most medical problems in camp were related to inadequate sanitation. There was a brief discussion of the unsatisfactory food situation in camp, and difficulty of monitoring its distribution and quality. VOLAGS were asked to increase supplementary feedings. Adjournment.

Such a meeting reveals some of the raw edges of a cross cultural undertaking, illustrating both the impotence of the international community here, and that reluctance of the Lao to engage our issues, which has always confounded the Western mentality.

Amazingly, the place continues to function. In fact, the confusion offers abundant opportunities for organized, motivated people to recognize needs and find solutions on small, manageable scales. There is no assurance that a massive, highly organized effort would work any better. Our history in Southeast Asia teaches that.

Amazingly, too, neither the consuming demands of bare survival, nor the awesome inefficiency of this place, seem able to destroy the easy grace of the Lao life style. They still manage to enjoy themselves. You see them dress up as best they can for a family promenade around camp. They organize elaborate baci ceremonies for friends and relatives leaving for the new life. They dance the traditionat *lamvong*, and listen to rock on their transistor radios. They go to the Buddhist *wat* or to one of the half-dozen churches in camp. They save up for an occasional visit to Nongkhai (the building chief has two passes to town to rotate among his residents). And they do nothing, a skill the West is rediscovering.

But the Lao are also changing. They have that refugee gleam about them. They are at a level of intense motivation to learn new ways. They will learn from the Western impulse to act, as surely we must learn from the Asian impulse to flow.

11
Camp Kids
Erik

Kids are the most abundant resource in the Refugee Camp. Many of them have a bad case of the universal childhood problem—there's nothing to do.

I suppose it's natural that camp kids like to make fun of us four *falang* kids. Kristine has it the worst. The teenage boys shout "phu sao" (marriageable young lady), and the little kids shoot water pistols at her, and pinch her to see if this blond kid is real. Mali doesn't get it as bad because she looks Lao. I get some heckling, but not much, and Mark is so friendly with everybody that I don't think anyone bothers him.

I have many special friends here among all age groups. It's easier to make friends with the younger kids. By the time they are in their early teens, Lao kids are considered adults, even though they may look like ten-year-olds, and sometimes act like it. I have some friends among kids my age (14), and I like Lao kids.

There is one big elementary school here and several smaller schools, operated by different church groups. But most kids don't go to school. That's because there isn't enough room, or they can't afford it, or both. The schools teach the three R's to all ages of kids, but not much beyond that. There are also some one-room schools, run as businesses in little shacks, mostly teaching English to adults.

Lots of little kids just seem to wander around looking for things to do. They have no toys like we think of toys. But they can make toys out of anything, especially the disposable items from the hospital. I think their favorite game is shooting rubber bands, preferably at a *falang*.

Some kids have jobs. The younger ones help their parents, if they have a stall in the market or some other little business. A lot of girls have steady work carrying their younger siblings around, and probably do more parenting than their parents do. Many of the older kids try to compete for the grown-up jobs. Sometimes you see a kid no older than twelve pedaling a *samlar*, maybe even with a younger brother riding along to help push up the hills.

But most of these premature adults still like to do the kinds of things kids do. Sometimes, it's strictly a Lao thing, like walking around with two-inch beetles that make a strange buzzing noise. Other times, it's hanging around, like we all do, bored with waiting for the next chapter to start. But there are few losers among them. Despite the lack of food and education, the kids in camp are definitely surviving.

Bounsu

Bounsu is happy. He wasn't always this way, but now he is. He went from no hope to sky-high hopes.

Everyone had abandoned him. His parents were dead, and his stepmother had kicked him out of the house. He had nowhere to go. His own country, Laos, offered no hope, for the Communists had destroyed his desire to stay there. He had heard the whispers about freedom "on the other side," about the chance for a new life, maybe in a rich country like America. His only chance, he decided, was to try to cross the Mekong river and face whatever there was on the other side.

Bounsu was a very small, stunted boy. Nobody believed that he was seventeen. He had always been a sickly child. And when food became more scarce, after the Communists came, he hardly grew at all.

Bounsu swam alone one night. The shots he heard were far away, but he was still terrified. It was the dry season, and the river was low. So was his strength. He barely reached the other side.

He was picked up by Thai border patrols and several days later transferred to Sokoto, the detention center at Nongkhai. In the crowd there he met an old friend who let the tired boy share his sleeping mat. But there was little food and much disease at Sokoto, and Bounsu was getting sicker. His friend took him to the little clinic, and there they decided to transfer him to the hospital in the refugee camp across the road.

Bounsu got his own bed, a nice wooden platform with a mat on it. It was right next to the feeding station. And the *falang* doctors held long discussions at his bedside (in their own language), and gave him medicines.

When I first met Bounsu I didn't know his name. He was the boy in bed 34 who'd eat huge amounts of whatever you gave him. He was always smiling. It was not surprising that he became a favorite of the staff. We all helped him learn English. He was very smart and always learning.

Before long a volunteer couple had agreed to be Boun-su's foster parents in the States. But their tour ended before Bounsu had cleared all the immigration hurdles. He saw them off at the train station. If he doubted his dream, he never showed it.

Bounsu was well enough to leave the hospital. One of the Lao nurses asked him to move in with their family.

One day we invited him home with us for lunch. We must have seemed strange. We sat on chairs instead of mats, we cooked with bottled gas instead of charcoal—and we talked back to our parents. He must have wondered how children could be so disrespectful, but he liked us and we enjoyed being together. Bounsu became my best Lao friend. He came home with us often.

Then we left, and Bounsu held his smile as he waved us off. A month later he got his clearance. He came to Minneapolis. Seeing him come down our driveway in Eden Prairie is a moment I'll never forget. We saw a lot of each other during the summer. This kid may have been sickly before. But you could tell that he was thriving in his new world. Then he flexed with one more change, moving with his foster family when they got a new job.

We've promised to visit each other. Dad told him that in ten years he expects DOCTOR Bounsu to volunteer for a stint at the Nongkhai refugee camp. We all laughed. But none of us doubted it.

12

Immigrants

Behind the Thai camp commander's building at Nongkhai is the large open pavilion that dominates life in the camp. This is the interview center, where refugees are screened and processed for resettlement, mostly to the United States, but also to other countries such as France, Canada, Australia, and China.

The pavilion is ringed and criss-crossed by ropes and fences and barricades that try to give a little order to the press of waiting, anxious refugees inside. It's crowded outside, too, with people endlessly checking the lists of names on the wall that may summon them for the next step in the processing. The place is as bleak and poignant as an Ellis Island.

At the center of this scene are three or four refugee families, each facing a young American across a card table. The stakes in these faltering interviews are incredibly high, and their faces show it. The Americans have been hired locally. They usually speak some Thai or Lao, and also have interpreters with them. Their job is to piece together a coherent file about a refugee family, on which the Embassy in Bangkok and the INS (US Immigration and Naturalization Service) can make some decisions.

It is a complicated process. As in Maha Chanty's case, a refugee first comes to the pavilion to register, filling out a form with basic biographic information. Then comes the pre-screening interview with all family members present. Then the file goes to Bangkok where the information is verified against information on people who worked for the Americans, for the Royal Lao Government, or against them. If everything checks out, there will be at least one more preparatory interview with the family, and then the case is turned over to the INS for a final interview. About once a month an INS team comes to Nongkhai. These interviews are more of a formality than the earlier ones. They end with the lucky refugee getting his T-number authorizing resettlement to the United States. By this time, up to a year may have passed since registration—and more hurdles remain.

The case now goes into the computer at the American Council of Voluntary Agencies (ACVA) in New York, where it stays the weeks or months until a suitable sponsor for the family is located in some American community.

Meanwhile the refugees must pass a medical screening. If there are changes, such as the birth of a child, there is a further delay, while the paperwork catches up.

When Bangkok is notified that a sponsor is lined up, the case goes to ICM (Intergovernmental Committee for Migration) which arranges travel to the United States, usually by air charter. The refugees go by bus from Nongkhai to one of the transit centers near Bangkok, where they wait several days or weeks.

And then, suddenly, comes a wanton storm of change

Opposite page: Refugee shopkeeper

that can choke the mind—encounters, often for the first time, with an airplane, and a western toilet, and an overweight person, and a million other wonders.

New Hope, Minnesota

During the nineteen sixties, in Laos, we knew a young nurse who trained and worked at the Vientiane Hospital. Her name was Sawie.

One night in October, 1979, Sawie slipped quietly down to the Mekong river, near Vientiane, and swam half-way across toward the Thai side. In mid-stream, as arranged, she was picked up by a boat from Thailand, and delivered, eventually, to the Lao refugee camp at Nongkhai, where she paid her pilots 4,000 *baht* ($200) for services rendered.

When we came to Nongkhai, we found Sawie working at the camp hospital. She became the chief nurse in the outpatient clinic. She registered for resettlement to the United States with her three sisters and a niece, who had come to Nongkhai before her.

On a summer day in 1980, one of the Americans at the interview center thought she smelled a rat. These four sisters didn't have the same name, and they didn't even look alike. She said their story was a lie. She interviewed them separately to probe for inconsistencies. She asked the name of the family dog, and what kind of cigarettes the father smoked. They passed.

One afternoon, in October 1980, a delegation from the Crystal Free Church of New Hope, Minnesota, assembled at the airport to meet Sawie and family, and to be their sponsors. (We were at the airport, too, and cried unabashedly when they came off the plane.)

Sawie has no U.S. credentials for nursing, so she started working as an interpreter at a hospital, and has applied and been accepted at a nursing school to begin her training all over again. Two of the sisters are in full-time English language training, and take in sewing on the side. They get some harassment from other refugees, whose sponsors have put them on welfare. The younger sister and the niece are in school. The sponsors are providing an apartment, and whatever food, clothing, chauffeuring, and hand-holding the family needs until it is self-sufficient. This is more than most sponsors are asked to give, but this group feels it can do it.

Sawie and her sponsors were brought together by the International Institute of Minnesota, an affiliate of the American Council for Nationalities Service. It was their second placement with the Crystal Free Church. Since the first one had been a very difficult case, the Institute was trying now to give this group a turn at what looked like an easy winner.

But that first case was also turning out better than many had hoped, according to Jerry Wilson, the General Mills food engineer who heads the refugee committee at Crystal Free Church. The family had arrived more than a year ago—a young Hmong couple, both about 20, with a four-month-old baby, rushed here on short notice because the mother urgently needed open heart surgery. They were like two frightened children.

The mother was hospitalized for three months before she was strong enough for surgery. The father was started in English training. When the mother finally came home, the church was geared up for a prolonged home care program. And then, abruptly, with the herding instinct that most immigrants have shown, the family moved away to live with an unemployed uncle in St. Paul.

But the New Hope group has stayed in contact with the family. The father now has a job, working the second shift as a janitor. The mother is pregnant again. They are speaking some English, and they seem to be quite happy living with two other Hmong families in a two bedroom apartment.

Resettlement

The United States has been accepting refugees from Southeast Asia at the rate of 14,000 a month. By the fall of 1980 about 400,000 of them were living in all of the United States, some 140,000 in California, 37,000 in Texas, and between ten and twenty thousand in the states of Washington, Pennsylvania, Illinois, Minnesota, Oregon, New York, Virginia, and Louisiana.

How are they doing? And what are they going to do with the rest of us? From the day they arrive, each refugee family acts out a series of answers to such questions.

We went to the airport to meet a public health nurse and her family from the Nongkhai camp. Until they escaped across the Mekong in 1979, they had never left Laos. She was an expert in skills like creating nutritious baby food over a charcoal fire in an outdoor village setting. She had never used a flush toilet, or ridden an airplane, or slept in a bed raised off the floor.

We saw her peering hopefully at the faces meeting her plane. She seemed much smaller than when we had known her in Nongkhai. Her face lit up as she spotted us. The children looked tired and frightened. Ahead of them was an old Hmong couple, in rubber sandals, who rushed tearfully into the arms of their warmly dressed, Americanized-looking relatives.

We led the way toward the baggage pick-up—and walked blithely onto the escalator. Our friends watched carefully. Then they spoke to the children to encourage them. No one faltered stepping on or off. And we had not thought to remember that they would never have seen such a contraption.

Just before we were to leave the airport, we noticed a tight circle of Hmong bodies standing silent and tense in the baggage area. They had arrived on the same plane. But they had not been met. Here they were in their chosen country, alone, and lacking even the limited English that our friends had. They looked as worried, and as fully alert, as if they were about to swim the Mekong. We approached and spoke in Lao. The father answered. They had relatives in Minnesota. We made a phone call (another inexplicable contraption). And we arranged for the resettlement worker who was with us to stay with the Hmong family, while we helped the sponsors to deliver the nurse and her family to their new home.

From such beginnings, each refugee family enacts its own drama. Their gaps in understanding things about our way of life that we take for granted are only sub-plots. The main drama is the astonishing adaptation that these refugees are able to make to a drastically different culture.

• A Minnesota farm family pledged to share their home with a Hmong refugee family, "until they become self-sufficient." The Hmong understood, and pitched right in. The first afternoon they came to the kitchen with their contribution to the family supper—a sack of squirming live squirrels they had caught in the woods, presumably by hand. . .

• A standard joke among refugees, according to one who has been here several months, is that the Americans haven't figured out how the bus system works. . .

• On a sub-zero day, we watched the six children of our

refugee friends, here about a year, running from their prized used car to the apartment, none of them with gloves on, but each happily clutching an ice cream cone. . .

• At a junior high school in St. Paul, every name on the honor roll is a Hmong name . . .

• On the Board of Directors of Minnesota International Health Volunteers is a successful plant agronomist—who four years ago arrived as a refugee from Laos and got a first job stuffing seed envelopes on the assembly line. . .

• The hard part, says a veteran of six years in our society, is learning to live with children who talk back to their parents. . .

There are, of course, many other variations to the plot, including, for some, a much slower adaptation to our society, and a prolonged reliance on welfare.

The Deadliest Crossing

And what does our culture see in the refugee family that walks off the plane? We rarely see the copers. Quite understandably, we see a pitiful collection of strange humanity, utterly unprepared to function in our society.

But volunteers who have seen them in the refugee camps come home with an overwhelming impression: These people can cope. They have proved their resourcefulness. And such human qualities run far deeper than a person's own culture.

Is our airport image, then, just a mirage from across the cultural gap? Not entirely. The transition into our society is still a highly vulnerable crossing. There are the obvious risks—the shocks of entering an incredibly complex and expensive culture, with a new language, new values, etc. But there is more.

There is the reality that the refugees must begin here by being far more dependent on others than they have ever been before—this from people who have arrived here mainly because they were the more self-sufficient ones. And then comes our welfare system, where the rewards for remaining dependent can exceed the wildest dreams of affluence in refugees who have known only the survival level. This is the final trap in the long journey to freedom, and it can be as terminal as swimming the Mekong.

What Should We Do

There is no easy way to titrate the level of support that is best for a given refugee. They all need help to get started, but no two are alike. Their need for our friendship and advice is often as deep as their need for training or financial support.

The critical element in meeting such needs is the army of volunteers who serve as sponsors of the refugees in all our communities. They are the refugee policy of the United States. Their consensus gives meaning to our Refugee Act and our public appropriations. They give the intimacy that can bond a new American.

Our impression is that we usually underestimate in the refugees the level of their personal motivation to make good in our country. For example, where our conventional wisdom is to teach job and language skills first and look for work later, many newly arrived refugees are ready to try doing both at the same time.

Much more language training and orientation to Western ways could be accomplished in the camps overseas, where intensely motivated refugees are waiting for the chance to immigrate. This would not require a massive program. A society that can field health volunteers can also field a rotating cadre of language volunteers in the refugee camps.

And we should be patient. Most of our refugee forefathers took a generation or more to learn the language and be absorbed into the society. The current batch is getting more help, and moving along much faster.

Finally, we believe the most useful thing we can do for refugees, and for ourselves, is to share their unbounded faith in the American Dream.

PART THREE

Health Care

13
Camp Medicine

"February 5: We have several epidemics at present, the biggest one being malaria. Half the hospitalized adults have falciparum malaria. We also have epidemics of measles, chicken pox, and mumps. We hospitalize many kids with bloody diarrhea, but so far haven't had the lab back-up to find the cause."

"February 17: On starting rounds tonight, I was horrified to see a dying child, marasmic on admission earlier in the day, now fifteen percent dry from profuse diarrhea. I rushed to the station. Fortunately Debbie happened to poke her head in on a Sunday drive. I grabbed a 25 scalp vein needle, she grabbed a metriset and D1/3S—all we had. I asked the father for permission to put a needle in a scalp vein. He cringed: I was breaking a taboo. 'Just a small one, please,' he said. Through that little vein went 100 cc in an hour. There began a feeble cry; then he moved, then he urinated. Potassium! There was none on the ward, but I grabbed the one vial I had in my bag. So it goes."

"February 28: Since the fire, three cats have been sneaking into the hospital. On call this week, I was trying to sleep on the cot in the area we call Central Supply, at the end of the pediatric ward. I could hear babies crying all night. At 5 a.m., I woke to the most outlandish 'baby' shrieks, and leapt to the ward. Two cats were fighting. And the patients were laughing."

The practice of medicine in a refugee camp has its special flavor. But it is fairly typical of the state of medicine for most of mankind. And it can give a westerner a dimension of a modern medical education that is rarely available, or even understood, at major medical centers.

Organization

The delivery of health care at Nongkhai, as in most developing country health care sites, involved a complex series of channels.

The Thai government operated the refugee camps through its Ministry of the Interior, conducted its health programs through its Ministry of Health, and channeled medical supplies through the Thai Red Cross. Thailand was struggling to cope honorably with a refugee flood that threatened to overwhelm it. The help of the world community was most welcome, so long as the life of the refugees was no less harsh than that of the Thai villagers around them, and the camps stayed grim enough not to become magnets for more refugees.

External assistance was channelled from other governments, through the UN High Commission for Refugees (UNHCR), to the Thai government, to the refugees. The UNHCR also had responsibility for coordinating the vast array of foreign voluntary agencies (VOLAGS) that were in Thailand to help the refugees.

At Nongkhai, the International Rescue Committee (IRC) had been designated the coordainting VOLAG for health programs. IRC had pioneered the Nongkhai program starting in 1976, maintaining a staff of several expatriate doctors and nurses, and whatever Lao doctors and nurses were available in the refugee population. The IRC, in turn, was delegating some of the health care assistance to other groups, such as MIHV and BASE (a Belgian health team).

The hospital was an open tin-roofed structure with a 20-bed adult ward and a 30-bed pediatric ward. The beds were wooden platforms with straw mats on them. There was a nursing station and small emergency and delivery rooms. An adjoining building held an outpatient department and a small lab and pharmacy. Across camp a third building housed a dental clinic and several small public health programs. These facilities served a camp population of about 30,000 refugees.

The actual delivery of health care at the hospital was in principle, and to a remarkable degree in practice, a function of the Lao refugee staff, with the expatriates serving primarily as back-ups and consultants. The Lao had their own hierarchy, as mysterious to outsiders as were the Thai and the expatriate hierarchies. But it set much of the tone of what would or would not be accomplished on the wards and in the clinics.

There were two levels of Lao doctors. Some had gone to the new medical school in Vientiane, which approximated a western medical education, at least in total years of schooling. Most, however, had taken four years of medical training after ten years of primary and secondary education. Nurses had six years of primary school and two years of nursing education. Very few of the Lao spoke English or French, and very few of the expatriates spoke Lao.

Not surprisingly, expatriate health workers at Nongkhai faced major barriers of communication. Language was not the biggest obstacle, since it could be bridged, at least crudely, by interpreters. The cultural gap was much harder to span. The Lao taboo against touching the head is one example. Even the foundation of western medicine, to save life at all cost, could be shaky in a culture that, far more than ours, saw death as a welcome release from the testings of life.

The official camp hospital and clinic was only a small part of the practice of medicine in the camp. It shared the stage with a rich assortment of other practitioners. There were thatch-hut pharmacies whre any drug, expired or not, was available without a prescription. There were private "clinics," mostly selling injections at about a dollar a shot. There were traditional healers of many sorts—herbalists, exorcists, and religious guides. The camp hospital and clinic was, for most of our patients, the second, third, or fourth stop, after having dabbled both with modern pharmacomania and a few traditional healing modalities.

Referrals

With our lack of X ray, surgical facilities, or 24-hour nursing coverage, patients needing more specialized diagnoses or treatment were referred into the Thai health care system.

Most of them went to the 260-bed Nongkhai Provincial

Hospital, the busy, unpretentious, but remarkably effective referral center for the Province. The eight or nine Thai doctors on the staff were young and overworked, but did what they could for the refugees. Expatriate doctors from the camp reciprocated by making weekly rounds with them both in pediatrics and medicine.

Referrals to Nongkhai could usually be made routinely, with the UNHCR absorbing the cost. If something more sophisticated was needed, the red tape and delay could be endless, and patients often died while awaiting referral. That was the fate of a beautiful 20-year-old mother with a fast growing facial tumor, whose story is told on page 105.

Likewise, there was little hope of treatment for patients with mental illness. The Thai had far too few mental health facilities for their own citizens. In the camp, demented refugees were usually cared for by their relatives and were sometimes chained.

Health Status

The medical records at the Nongkhai refugee hospital gave very little hint of the health status in camp. It was not only their hopeless mixture of French, English and Lao. They tended to record symptoms, rather than diagnoses, because we rarely had the lab, X ray, or consultant back-up to confirm or deny diagnostic suspicions.

During the week of January 15-22 we kept track of the likely diagnoses of all hospitalized patients.

Among adults, 55% had falciparum malaria, 10% had pulmonary infections (possible tuberculosis), 5% had measles, 5% had beri-beri, and 25% had other illnesses, including cardiac failure, dysentery and gunshot wounds.

Among children 40% had diarrhea and dehydration, 35% had pulmonary infections, 25% had stage III protein energy malnutrition, 16% had malaria, 20% had fevers of unknown origin, and 10% had other diseases, including measles, burns, and parasites. Some of the above were multiple diagnoses.

Many refugees came from relatively isolated villages in Laos and, as a result, had little immunity to common childhood illnesses such as measles and chicken pox. Measles in the camp was common, not only in adults, but also in young infants, suggesting a lack of adult immunity.

Epidemics of falciparum malaria, diphtheria, giardiasis, amoebiasis, and cholera occurred in early 1980. Tuberculosis was rife. Tetanus, pertussis, and all the usual parasitic infestations were common.

Malnutrition

But the most pressing health problem at Nongkhai, as in most communities in less developed countries, was that of malnutrition. Ironically, it was also a problem that could be overlooked. The conventional wisdom had been that, since one saw relatively few cases of full-blown marasmus or kwashiorkor at Nongkhai, malnutrition was not a major problem here.

But children who looked to be about eight years old turned out to be twelve, and what seemed to be three-year-olds were actually six.

Weights and heights had not been routinely recorded in the past in camp clinics. So we did a nutrition survey, measuring factors such as height, weight, head circumference, skin fold thickness, and length of time in the camp, of 301 children, mostly in the outpatient clinic.*

The results were startling. In their weight-to-height ratio—the most accurate indicator of nutritional status—twenty-six percent of the children fell below the fifth percentile. This survey, and others by Catholic Relief Services and Food for the Hungry, confirmed the clinical impression that there was a serious problem of chronic malnutrition and stunting among children at the Nongkhai camp.

A poor state of nutrition also meant a state of lowered resistance to infection. It explained in part why we had such a steady parade of epidemics of infectious diseases to crowd our hospital wards.

Prevention

The camp medical program had focused mainly on caring for sick people, with little time left for preventive programs like nutrition and immunization and sanitation. We were in the classic bind of many health programs in less developed countries, overwhelmed with glaring needs for immediate attention, yet knowing that what had to be done was to sit back, take a deep breath, and say, "I'm taking time out to plan an immunization program, even though someone might die while I do so."

Fortunately, such a resolve was evolving in 1980 among expatriate health workers at Nongkhai. We would try as hard to help refugees be healthy, as we did to treat their illnesses. It helped that there was a brief surge in our

*See Karen Olness, M.D., and Erik Torjesen: "Nutritional and Health Status in a Lao Refugee Camp," in MINNESOTA MEDICINE, 63:411, 1980.

resources during this period, although that also meant that the test of our resolve had been deferred.

For the present, the wards were still jammed, especially the thirty beds on the pediatric side. But most of us knew that six or eight pediatric beds would be plenty for a camp of 30,000—if only we could keep the momentum going on prevention.

And a healthier breed of refugees would arrive for re-settlement.

14
Fire at the Soon Karen

"The Soon burned down last night . . . in forty-five minutes . . . most of it's gone!"

Those incredible words came from Winnie Kaetzel, the missionary, who had just interrupted an early breakfast at our house. The Kaetzel's headquarters in Bangkok had phoned in the middle of the night. The news had reached there before it reached our houses six kilometers from camp. We rushed to the *Soon*.

Here are my diary notes:

February 16

In retrospect, the whole day seems like a mirage—the smoldering ruins where yesterday we walked, the dazed patients, the crying Lao nurses, the sense that there is no adequate way to respond to a disaster that has hurt twenty thousand people.

When we arrived, the hospital wards were empty. During the fire, patients had yanked their intravenous lines and run, and wisely so, for the fire actually singed the hospital. By ten a.m., most had returned. There was no water, no electricity. Hakon went back to town and brought all the clean water from our house. Mali stayed there to boil more.

As soon as we had a semblance of a treatment station, people began coming in, mostly with burns, or with cuts in their feet from running through the ruins. A six-year-old girl was rushed in, bleeding profusely, knifed just below her left ear—over food. Almost no one had eaten since last night, and food relief efforts were not yet visible.

Sawie, the OPD head nurse, was dressed in a black trench coat she had apparently grabbed as she ran. She and her family, like everyone else, had escaped with what they could carry. It had been a chilly night sitting in the field. Those who had a coat or a sweater treasured it. Hakon brought out our remaining suitcase of extra clothing. It went fast.

Kris was pouring boiling water in the hospital and spilled some on her foot. So she had a burn like everyone else. We came home at two for a short break, and I dressed her foot. On the way back to camp, I stopped at the Nongkhai hospital where several of our patients had ended up. They were okay.

Back at the OPD, we treatred an unending line of patients, mostly for minor injuries. The Lao staff was too dazed to help much, but many of them were trying. The lab and pharmacy managed to keep going. A team of expatriate volunteers from the Ban Vinai camp arrived to help. Part of them agreed to form a night shift. Dr. Speert took them out to eat. Between five and seven p.m. I admitted six patients. I went home around nine. Was the day real?

February 17

Another gruelling day. I felt drained by the pathos everywhere. The Ban Vinai volunteers stayed with us all day. Nursing was more of a shambles than usual. But I was surprised at how many Lao nurses tried to help, in spite of having been burned out, and the need to find shelter for their families.

Hakon went out to buy sleeping mats and mosquito nets. I gave out twenty sets to the nurses and to new patients. I stayed at camp all day, except for one trip to Nongkhai hospital to buy more tetanus toxoid. Granola bar for lunch.

On the wards, patients filled all the beds and much of the floor. In the OPD, patients were pouring in all day.

At three o'clock, the Thai camp commander was carried in, acutely ill with abdominal pain. I started an IV. I worried about pancreatitis, a perforated ulcer. His hemoglobin was 11. He told me he had not eaten since the fire. I persuaded him to be transferred to the Nongkhai hospital.

Next came a UN official from Bangkok, also with an acute abdomen . . . and then an American nurse.

It's remarkable how this stress spills onto the expatriates, even though we have lost nothing. Part is fatigue, part is confusion. But part must be the Aidos and Nemesis that Toynbee wrote about—the shame and indignation of the "haves" when direclty confronted with the "have-nots."

Home at ten. One of the Ban Vinai doctors took night call. I'll be on tomorrow night.

15

Children's Graveyard Karen

In Memory of Phenphonevisith

He was cuddled by the Lao staff, and by the visiting Thai Dean of the medical school, and by big Leon, the sanitarian from Oregon, and by Sara Lawton and her husband David Speert, who had planned to be his sponsors, and by Toshiko, the lovely Japanese volunteer who coaxed him to eat—and by me. We all loved the sad faced 20-month-old boy, who always reached out to us, but who never smiled. His name was Phone, short for Phenphonevisith.

Phone suffered from marasmus (severe malnutrition), and many complicating infectious diseases. His mother, age 20, was also in the hospital, dying of a facial tumor. Phone's young father tended him day and night on our ward. One cause of his malnutrition may have been the depression in the family, and among the relatives who came visiting, over the impending death of his once beautiful mother. Her consultation in Bangkok had been approved too late. They sent her back to us to die.

After several weeks in the hospital, Phone was just beginning to enjoy eating again. Then his father became frightened by the cholera epidemic, and the many cholera patients who were contaminating the ward. He asked to take Phone home. He took with him a supply of vitamins, and supplement, and Ovaltine, which we had bought for him.

Four days later, they came back. Phone was dehydrated and in shock. Transfusions and antibiotics were too late. Phone died at ten one Thursday morning. I was at the other end of the camp, doing a well-baby clinic at the time of his death. The father found me there, gave me the news, and asked if we would bring the yellow pick-up to drive Phone's body to the children's graveyard. I agreed.

Children's Graveyard? I had been here four months, and I didn't know about a Children's Graveyard.

That very morning, in Hakon's English and orientation class for Lao doctors, they were exploring attitudes about death . . . that here many children died, and not much was made of it, but in their new professional settings, the death of a child would be far more of an outrage than the death of an aged person. At that point I walked in on the class and said Phone was dead. The doctors read our faces, and the lesson was real. All of us decided to escort Phone to the Children's Graveyard.

Outside, the young father had assembled relatives and friends, some of whom carried shovels. Three Lao doctors and Erik were joining us. At high noon, in an ambient temperature of 106 degrees, we stood outside the pediatric ward as the father carried Phone's body into the back of the pick-up. We drove off, still wondering where we would arrive.

From the camp gate, we drove a short distance east,

and stepped out. Flies swarmed around the truck. The sun was unmerciful. Single file, we picked our way across the camp dump—across broken glass, rotting garbage, tin cans. One of the lady doctors held her parasol delicately, trying to shield me as well as herself. Slowly, the horrible truth dawned on me. The Children's Graveyard was part of the camp dump.

"Why don't they go to the *Wat* (temple)?" I asked one of the doctors.

"Because they don't have any money, and besides there isn't room for another funeral in the *Wat* today."

I cringed. "I am walking through a dump to a baby's funeral." It was miserably hot, but I noticed little except a feeling of failure, and of anger over the preventable malnutrition in this camp.

After walking about half a kilometer, we came to an area on the edge of the dump that was less cluttered, but it had scores of little mounds, each representing a dead child from this camp. Some of the mounds had bamboo sticks or branches on top to mark them. Most of them had little belongings of the child set on top. There were bottles of medicine, baby shoes, clothing, bottles, milk formula cans.

The earth here was sandy. These mounds had to be from this dry season— from the past six month only. This meant that many children died outside the camp hospital, and were brought here.

Phone's father selected a site, and the digging began. The sun beat down. A few feet from us were heaps of refuse. We stood silently. After a while the father said we didn't need to wait. We took our cue and walked back, across the dump, and away from the death of a child.

So many factors entered into the death of this beautiful boy—his mother's malignancy, his father's depression, the

rejection of our proposed night feeding program, the mal-
distribution of food, the cholera epidemic, and factors we
are missing.

Phone's mother died a few days later. We took her
body to the Christian church. Two months later, the father
and his younger brother left camp to start a new life in the
United States.

Their sponsors may never hear the story of Phone and
his mother. The Lao rarely talk about past tragedies. And
by now the rains have come and gone, and Phone's grave
has surely washed away, along with the others, and new
ones will have come.

But now we know where the children's graveyard is.
And volunteers go out there from time to time, to sharpen
their resolve. And the graveyard is getting smaller. At this
writing there has been much improvement in feeding programs for children, and in immunization and sanitation
programs. There are fewer deaths of children at Nongkhai.

Thank you, Phone.

16
Health and Culture   Karen

The babel of culture and hierarchies shaping health care at Nongkhai could be unnerving for the western mentality. It was easy to forget that complexities such as these were much more the rule than the exception in most health care settings— and that the incongruities of our own health care system could be as baffling to refugees arriving in the West, as the system here was to us.

It was of some help to us that we had lived five years in Laos during the sixties, and had even found a Lao flower, our daughter Mali. But we knew we were still missing the meaning of much of what went on around us. And so were most of our peers. There were daily misunderstandings between expatriates and refugees, each of whom tended, like most humans, to project their own culture onto others.

Some of the Lao customs related to birth and child raising gave us vivid illustrations of the gaps that can exist between health cultures.

Traditionally, half the babies born in Laos have died

before the age of two. We had seen this sad phenomenon in the sixties, and it probably continues to the present except in some of the more wealthy families. It may explain the belief among the Lao that a child is not a complete person, and therefore not worthy of a name, until age two. A common name for Lao babies is "E Noi"—Little One.

Many parents believe that bestowing a beautiful name may cause bad spirits to desire the child. Likewise, it is a taboo to praise the beauty of an infant, lest a bad spirit notices and decides to take the child. A generation ago, loving grandmothers would plot to keep strong and beautiful babies hidden for the first year or two. At Nongkhai, unwitting refugee workers who had praised the beauty of a baby could be blamed if the infant later died.

In the refugee camp, as in Laos and in most communities of the world, births usually occurred at home. Whether at home or at our hospital, childbirth happened calmly, as a natural event. We saw little of the stress found in American labor rooms, except among the more educated Lao women. If the infant was delivered at home, the custom was to cut the umbilical cord with a piece of sharp bamboo, and then rub the cord with buffalo dung. Hence, neonatal tetanus was a common problem.

A strong tradition—still practiced by 90 percent of Lao women, according to a female Lao physician friend—is that the mother, for one month following delivery of her baby, must sit by a charcoal fire, eat only rice and some salt, and drink only water or tea. This made it very difficult to persuade parents to hospitalize newborns with sepsis or other diseases, since the mother couldn't leave the fire. Sometimes, though, we could satisfy both Lao and Western imperatives by making an electric burner available several times a day to a new mother in the hospital.

Shortly after birth, the Lao infant would be blessed at a baci ceremony. The baci is a beautiful animist ritual, performed at all manner of special occasions. Participants sit around a floral centerpiece, first for a Pali incantation to the wandering souls to return to the body, and then for individual expressions of good fortune spoken while tying cotton threads around the wrist of a recipient. These lucky threads were often seen on the wrists of newborns and ill children.

The Lao consider their feet to be the unclean part of the body, much as the genitalia sometimes have an unclean connotation in our culture. The head is sacrosanct, the holiest part of the body. The American who reaches out to pat the head of a Lao child is breaching etiquette, as is the one who proceeds to start an intravenous line in the head of an infant without asking permission.

To lay an infant down to sleep on his tummy is unheard of in the Lao tradition. I have wondered whether this could be related to the French colonial influence in Laos, because French babies also sleep only on their backs or sides.

Most Lao babies are breast fed. But during the past generation there has been some emulation of western mothers seen bottle feeding their babies. With unsterile bottles, filthy water, and no refrigeration, the results have often been disastrous. During the rigors of escaping from Laos, many mothers lost their milk. Then they bought sweetened condensed milk, diluted it excessively, and fed it in dirty bottles. There followed much infectious diarrhea and malnutrition, and sometimes death.

Rice is the basic food in Laos. They even use the same word, *khao*, to mean both rice and a meal. (The Chinese do likewise with their word, *fahn.*) When infants are two or three months old, mothers begin solids by chewing some rice and spitting it into the mouths of their babies. If breast milk has dried up, and there is no money for condensed milk, this can be the infant's only sustenance. By eight or nine months most Lao babies have learned to enjoy the wonders of sticky rice (glutinous rice), which is the favored variety in the Mekong Valley.

Unfortunately, rice tends to be the only weaning food. A Lao mother will not give eggs to a young child, because she believes that a child will not get his teeth if he eats eggs. Many Lao mothers do not know how to mince meats and vegetables and cook them in a rice soup. At the well-baby clinic, we set up demonstrations, by the Lao nurses, using traditional tools and fires. We offered tastes. Some mothers insisted their babies would never eat the stuff. But when the babies gobbled it eagerly during the demonstrations, many were convinced. And when the babies started looking bigger, better, and stronger, the mothers told others how to do it.

Lao children, like children in most cultures, like sweets, and these were far more available in the refugee camp than in the traditional cultures. Soft drinks were sold in a plastic bag, tied with a rubber band, with a straw sticking out. The teeth of camp children were much worse than we had seen in their traditional villages.

Lao children also snacked on many foods that Westerners would consider highly unusual—beetles, lizards, and roasted termite wings. Our daughter was bewildered one morning at our house, when we sent her out to sweep up after a termite swarm. A Thai neighbor woman rushed over to stop her, and delightedly gathered up the wings for one of her favorite delicacies.

The Lao, like most people in our world, cannot afford diapers for their babies. This leads to remarkably early toilet training, at least by Western standards. Mothers, not wishing to get their skirts wet or dirty, tune in to baby signals that urination or defecation is about to occur. Many times, while I was examining an infant in the OPD, the mother would suddenly scoop up the baby and run to the open trench outside our building. Never, in the refugee camp, or during the earlier years in Laos, did a Lao parent bring me a child with the complaint of bedwetting.

Lao parents indulge their young children far more than western parents do, and indulge their older children far less than we do. Babies and toddlers tend to be carried by their mothers almost every waking moment—until the day the next baby comes along. Then he is abruptly set aside. Unless there is an older sibling, or an aunt or grandmother, to cuddle the toddler, he tends to go into decline. Kwashiorkor, a form of severe malnutrition, got its name from an African tribal tongue. The phrase means "disease of the deposed child."

The Lao cannot comprehend some of our child raising customs. How can we bathe a child with a fever? Didn't our grandmothers tell us that was bad? (Mine did, and she may have been right.) Why do we feed a child with diarrhea? Well, just ten years ago, we believed, like the Lao, in starving the child with diarrhea. Why do we make the baby sleep away from his parents? And why don't we listen to what the grandmothers say about child raising? Aren't they the wisest?

And why do we feed our babies such strange foods? In fact, feeding customs for children in the United States have changed many times, and will surely continue to change. Some of the Lao customs may be nutritionally sounder than ours.

The Lao watched our family with great interest. Most

of the volunteers they saw were singles, so, for many of them, we were the first Western family they had met. They noted that our boys worked in day care, and fed the babies. They wondered why they saw the whole family pitching in with household chores. We did our own cooking? They had thought we were elite, and the elite in Laos always had servants. We explained that they won't have that in America.

There was much for them to ponder, on the verge of their drastic adjustment to a new culture. We showed them the sticky rice baskets we were taking back to the States. And we hoped they would like our Big Macs as much as we liked their sticky rice!

17
Health Outreach*

In my first exposure to international health, eighteen years ago, I landed in Laos "waving a stethoscope" and brimming with energy for curing the ills of "the developing world." My pre-departure orientation had been minimal. Fortunately, the on-site orientation lasted seven years, on two continents, and imprinted me to continue some studying and teaching in this field.

When I did it again in 1980, the stethoscope was still very busy. But there was more to energize us. My colleagues and I were determined to remember the principal lesson of the last few decades in third world health care, namely that amid overwhelming needs for acute care, success depends not so much on acute intervention as on efforts in education, prevention, and continuity of care. We were seized, also, with facilitating for students and grad-

---

*Portions of this chapter are adapted from an article, "A Health Outreach To A Refugee Camp: Perspectives for Would-Be Volunteers," by Karen Olness, M.D., in the April, 1981 issue of PEDIATRICS, published by the American Academy of Pediatrics.

uate professionals a more meaningful first exposure to international health than some of us had received. And by now we knew that, overall, we could expect to receive far more than we gave in this experience.

MIHV

Minnesota International Health Volunteers (MIHV) had evolved over many planning years among a group of health professionals, not limited to Minnesotans, who were interested in international health. They represented the private practice community, numerous Minnesota medical institutions, and the faculty of the International Health course at the University of Minnesota Medical School.

MIHV took as its broad objectives to help meet the long-term health needs of one or more third world communities, and, in these settings, to offer practical training and research opportunities in international health to accompanying medical students and graduate professionals, and to local health personnel.

MIHV's main resource was a coalescence of health volunteers, available for short-term overseas assignments, but committed to long-term planning and careful preparation before they went flying off to somewhere. The MIHV concept included extensive pre-departure orientation, relatively long overseas tours of three to six months duration, and the intention that volunteers would consider repeating their rotations every two or three years, as long as needed. Volunteers would be encouraged to bring their families with them overseas, conditions permitting.

This program was offered to the International Rescue Committee (IRC) in 1979 as a possibilty for one of its medical projects among refugees in Southeast Asia. IRC invited MIHV to establish a team of approximately two physicians, two nurses, and two medical students in the IRC program at the Lao refugee camp in Nongkhai, Thailand. The American Refugee Committee (ARC) agreed to provide part of the cost of transportation and living expenses for the MIHV team.

In mid-1980, the IRC asked MIHV to establish a second outreach, this time at Khao I Dang, the largest of the Cambodian refugee camps along the Thai border. MIHV would take responsibility for the IRC's pediatric program there, beginning in early 1981.

About Volunteers

The consensus among scores of health volunteers we met in Thailand was that, despite the inevitable frustrations of emergency programs, especially across cultures, their experience here was productive for the health of refugees, and a personal and professional highlight of their lives.

Such a consensus seems to have emerged wherever volunteers have taken hold, in our time, and all the times before us.

At refugee camps and similar transitory sites, it would be extremely difficult to assemble a permanent staff that could match the professional skill and experience that is available through rotating volunteers. With careful planning and preparation, many highly qualified people from the mainstream of the health professions are able to offer their services for rotations of three to six months, and to consider repeating such service from time to time. And if they can consider bringing their families (albeit at their own expense), that opens the prospect of volunteering even further.

The family aspect seems to have worked out just fine for us at Nongkhai. (My colleague, Professor John Murray, and his entire family had set us a worthy example with their many summers of significant service and research as volunteers in Africa.) All of our family became intensely involved in projects at the camp. And in a place like this, where most expatriates are singles, and most refugees are families trying to understand the world to which they will be resettled, just being seen as a western family can be quite important.

Our replacements here will span three generations. They are Dr. Arnold Anderson, the founder of Minneapolis Children's Hospital, his wife Rusk, and their two teenage daughters—plus their oldest son, Dr. Renner Anderson, his wife Dr. Martha Anderson, and their two toddler children.

The volunteers we meet in the refugee camps are a marvelous cross-section of the health professions. Some of them are young and relatively free of binding responsibilities at home. Others have discovered that their many professional, family, and financial obligations, still leave them the option to come here, at $300 a month for subsistence—plus an indescribable enrichment.

Volunteer Preparation

There can be no single curriculum for preparing overseas health volunteers. But there is wide agreement that the value of the outreach tends to vary rather precisely with the quality of the pre-departure preparation.

Most voluntary agencies offer some pre-departure

Opposite Page: Faces at Day Care Center

orientation for their volunteers. The program MIHV is developing in the Twin Cities meets every Friday night for thirteen weeks. This is probably longer than most, not only in terms of hours, but also in terms of the three-month time span during which a volunteer can prepare himself psychologically for the changes ahead. Each session starts with an hour of basic training in conversational Thai, Lao or Cambodian, followed by an hour of orientation and discussion about the work in the refugee camps. The emphasis is on cultural, rather than medical considerations.

None of the above, of course, will have anywhere near the impact of actually working in another culture. But it should increase the likelihood that the first overseas assignment will be a rich learning experience.

PART
FOUR

Five Months

18
Getting There

Erik

Most people get there by swimming the Mekong—dodging bullets and all that. A few of us fly in from America. Either way, getting to the Nongkhai Refugee Camp is likely to change your life.

Mom and Dad had been there before, so we had a bit of a clue to what we might find. That helped when people asked, "Why do you want to go there?" But it was different. We really didn't know why we were going until after we got there.

The big suitcases were already in the Aspen; we had loaded them the night before. So all we had to put in the Rodberg's Suburban was our carry-on luggage and, of course, ourselves. We set off in convoy for the Minneapolis-St. Paul airport.

Inside the terminal, we made a pile of our coats, boots, hats and gloves to be taken back to the house. There were cousins and aunts and uncles. Dr. Anderson and a medical student had brought two china barrels of medical supplies to go as excess baggage. Our checked luggage count was now 14, and by the time the six of us got on the plane, our carry-ons totalled 17. We left on time, at about 11:20 a.m., on Friday the 11th of January, 1980, on what seemed like the adventure of our lives.

We got to Seattle an hour late because of head winds, then waited three hours while they de-iced the plane, and then almost missed the connection in Tokyo. At Hongkong the airline gave us a nice hotel for five hours of sleep. But next morning we missed the flight to Bangkok because the time on the tickets was off by an hour. That gave us time for some sightseeing. We got to Bangkok that evening. Three days later we took the night train to Nongkhai.

Our family had been planning to do something like this for years. Fortunately, we knew five months in advance that we were going to Nongkhai. This gave us time to get used to the idea, and tell our friends about it. A lot of volunteers make spur of the moment decisions and leave without any preparation. I know that for a family of six that would be nearly impossible.

When we left, the media were fixated on blowing up the Cambodian situation. That confused people. Many times, after we painstakingly explained that we were going to help Lao refugees, the conversation would end with, "Well, good luck with the Cambodians."

When you leave for five months, you're not moving, and it's not a vacation. It's a totally new experience.

I've heard that the safest way to get there, if you have money, is to buy off the communist officials. That's not the way most people leave Laos. The majority simply swim the river. Now, during the dry season, that can look fairly simple. But when the rains come, it will be more of a feat. Bullets, of course, have no season.

19

Early Glimpses

In Southeast Asia, there are three seasons of the year. From November to February is the cool, dry season. March and April are the hot, dry season. From May until October is the rainy season. Our stay in Thailand, from January to early June, 1980, touched all the seasons.

This chapter is a roughly chronological selection of impressions from our journals and letters home during the cool months of January and February.

We've been here three weeks, and it seems like three months. We are happy and finding lots to do. Beth Porras, the IRC medical director, has outlined broad health objectives. She was the only expatriate doctor on the wards until Karen arrived. Erik has been helping Karen do a nutritional study of the kids, and it turns out there is a serious problem of chronic malnutrition here. Beth has asked the girls to help her start a day care center in the hospital to teach well-child skills. Mark has been helping me with English and orientation classes, which we have started for the Lao doctors and nurses. The level of disorganization in this camp is what you might expect—only worse. There is very little central purpose or direction to the international effort here. Individuals can only look for obvious needs and, if they have the interest, start tackling them (H.T.)

* * *

This is a place of peaks and valleys. There is the flush of success in the refugee who has made it safely across the Mekong, followed by long dreary months of waiting, and nursing that impossible dream of a new life somewhere.

Some of the valleys go all the way down.

The father looked passive at first, then anxious, then burst into tears as his son vomited blood. "This is all I have," he cried. "They killed my wife and the other two children, and now this one will die too." We transferred the boy to Nongkhai hospital. Two days later he was getting better, and I found the father standing asleep over the boy's bed, with the upper part of his body curled down on the crib mattress. There was no place for him to sleep. "Never mind," he said, "the boy is recovering." I knew he hadn't eaten all day. I gave him some money, and tried to couch it so he wouldn't lose face. "You must eat for the boy's sake; it's important that you eat."

I say, "Your child is sick from malnutrition." Tears flow down the mother's face. "I give what I have, but I know that's not enough. I don't have any money to buy food." Over and over I hear it. Where are the relief efforts going? What happens to the food? My emotions rage. The brains of this child are small. What does that mean for him, twenty years from now, trying to hack it in the States? And I know I can't answer these questions. (K.O.)

* * *

We have begun a night call schedule for the expatriates. Staying overnight on the ward is a special experience—awful in the physical sense, but very stimulating workwise, and always a learning experience. I was on last Sunday night, from four in the afternoon until about twelve-thirty on Monday.

The Lao doctor on call never appeared, but an off-duty colleague came by to visit, and helped with the patients, while we talked about medicine in the United States. We discovered a moribund baby, admitted that morning with diarrhea, and now in shock. We got an IV going, and the baby revived. She cried all night.

Late that evening, we sat around the nursing station and talked. Patients were on the sidelines, and soon joined in. They wanted to know about schools and jobs and farming in the United States. I wanted to reinforce the need for sterile techniques, and for giving patients their two a.m. meds, even if the custom had always been for the nurses to bed down at eleven. For them, and for me, this was one of those rare, unhurried occasions when you could speak across cultures, and be heard. (K.O.)

* * *

ALL MIHV PEOPLE WELL AND BUSY FOL-LOWING NONGKHAI CAMP FIRE. INFORM FRIENDS. LOVE.

Thanks for your cable. We haven't told many people, because no one around Minneapolis has heard anything about a fire at Nongkhai. We called AP and UPI, and they have nothing on it. We're glad you're well and busy.

* * *

We've been here six weeks, and we're pretty much settled into our Nongkhai house. We do dishes, clean house, work at the camp, ride bikes, read books and do school work. We have a short wave receiver, so we listen to news and music from the Voice of America in Washington.

You'd like the food here, though I find it too hot. Some dishes my dad can't even handle, and he was practically raised on red peppers. They mix chopped peppers with rancid fish sauce, and eat it like soup. Haahhh!!! (E.T.)

* * *

Last weekend I was in charge of the new feeding program in the hospital, and really enjoyed it. Up to now there hasn't been much of a system for refeeding the malnourished kids, and even the babies didn't get formula regularly. The kids eat like crazy.

The weather has been nice, 80-90 degrees, but soon the normal temperature will be over 100 degrees. A few days ago we had a freak rain storm. People said it was the hardest they'd seen. I hear you had a bit of that cold white stuff at home. Happy skiing, you scums. (E.T.)

* * *

Don't feel guilty telling me about your vacation. During our first month here, life was much less complex than at Children's, even though we had huge amounts of clinical work. We were only about four expatriates, working with a Lao staff of four doctors and about 25 nurses. Most of us spoke Lao or Thai, and things ran smoothly. In some ways it was like a vacation for me.

Well, this "institution" is now growing. In the past three weeks it has added two American doctors, a dentist, four nurses, an X ray tech, a social worker, two sanitarians, and a medical technologist. The extra hands were needed. But, unfortunately, only one spoke Lao. So, four interpreters were hired. But they had no background in medical terminology—Lao or English. Then the Lao nurses became angry because interpreters, with no medical background, were paid as much as they were. The nurses threatened to leave. The Americans began projecting their frustrations over communication onto the Lao staff. Recently, we have had a multitude of committee meetings, whereas, during the first month, we had only one. All interactions are now more complex. We are experiencing a psychic drain from the need to bring in more people. It's the same back home, of course. So enjoy your vacation. (K.O.)

20

Dear Colleague

These are excerpts from Karen's letters during March, April and May, 1980.

Greetings from hot, dusty Nongkhai. We are delighted with this site for an MIHV project. We are asking a favor of you. A returning volunteer is today hand-carrying to Seattle, and will then mail to you, a formaldahyde-fixed sequestra from the jaw of a five-year-old Hmong boy, some soft tissue (we hope), and, I am not entirely sure about this, a tooth. I hope you can help in establishing the diagnosis.

Why this comes to you, is as follows: A week ago a mother brought her boy to the OPD with a jaw that had been swelling for three months. They came from the miserable holding center down the road from camp. They had arrived there a week earlier in a group of 200 Hmong who had started out from their village in Northern Laos as a group of 500. At first the boy and his mother had been accompanied by the father, a six-year-old brother, and a two-week-old infant. During the two months of their escape through mountain jungles, the group was decimated by land mines and disease. One night, they knew the communist soldiers were near, and the crying children had to be sedated. The parents gave a potion to the baby, and also to the six-year-old, who was crying. Inadvertently, they gave too much. The two children died. And when they crossed the Mekong River, the father was shot and drowned.

As soon as she could, the grieving, malnourished mother brought the five-year-old here for help. We admitted him. The mass over the right lower jaw was rock hard, and I could see protuberances alongside the lower right molars. He had no particular adenopathy, but did have a large spleen. That would be common in this malaria-ridden population, and the boy did, in fact, have falciparum malaria as well as the jaw mass.

The drainage and biopsy was done at the Nongkhai Provincial hospital by a Thai surgeon and Chester Taylor, the oral surgeon volunteering here with IRC.

* * *

We had an influx of fourteen new American volunteers during the week before and week after the fire. I got the impression that 20,000 homeless Lao was less chaotic than fourteen unacculturated foreigners. Our first medical student is fluent in Thai, and he is like manna from heaven for the Lao doctors and nurses who are struggling to communicate with all the new *falang*. . . .

I am more than ever convinced that a pre-departure orientation plan, such as ours, is the key to effectiveness in this kind of program. There just aren't many Mace Goldfarbs around, who can adapt quickly in a new culture.

There is a constant parade of visitors and inspectors through the refugee camps, representing churches,

VOLAGS, US senators, etc., and conducting endless "needs assessments." Some days Hakon and I feel like we're back in the foreign service.

* * *

Last Sunday, we waited downtown in the 100 degree heat for two hours, trying to get a call through to Minneapolis. Then we cabled, asking MIHV to call us Friday night, your time. We waited three hours, in vain. . . .

Two days ago, we finally went ahead and bought the pick-up truck. Now we need the money! We used our family return travel funds to pay for the truck. . . .

We had an excellent MIHV meeting last night, the first time the team had assembled for a group discussion. We did a "right-wrong search." And we made a little wish list. We could use some paper cups for feeding patients. We never seem to have enough containers here. And what we have tends to go home with the patients who get better, because dishes are short everywhere in camp. Yesterday I used a urinal (clean) for feeding a patient. We also need plastic spoons. If we could get a donation of topical antifungals, it would help. We finally got enough benadryl. . . .

The quarterly report should be in the mail this week. We remain hot and happy, though I have a dripping nose cold, and Mark is recovering from measles. So far we've gotten only Minnesota-type illnesses—none of the intestinal upsets so usual for the *falang*.

* * *

Bob arrived on the 22nd. We had a message that he was coming on the 21st, and went to the train station on a false alarm. For all I know, Doyle could be on the train tonight.

Thanks again for the boxes. I resuscitated a newborn with the infant Laerdal two days after it arrived. Last night, at the Nongkhai Provincial Hospital, I assisted at an infant resuscitation and realized that they don't have the proper tubes and bags there, although they seem to understand the use of resuscitation equipment better than the staff at the camp. So I plan to share some of the equipment with them. . . .

The truck is a God-send. Delighted to hear that the Eden Prairie Rotary Club and Rotary International will buy it. Hakon will visit some of the Thai clubs to thank them.

* * *

Once again rushing to get this in the hands of someone leaving on the Bangkok train in an hour. All the boxes arrived on Sunday. Bob couldn't manage them all on the train when he came, so an IRC van brought them up from Bangkok. We had an unpacking party. Great happiness.

We've been following a family that Pop Buell asked us to check on, and have just learned that most of them are leaving Monday for Eagan, Minnesota. We gave them the black suitcase, that your friend had sent with his name inside. I'm sure they'll contact him. This family saved Pop's life years ago in Northern Laos. The father is still in prison in Laos, and they are leaving a family member in camp to wait for him, in case he makes it out.

* * *

Seems impossible to think of leaving this special place in seven weeks. We trust you will debrief the Speerts when they arrive. They will be sponsoring a foster son, age 17.

We got Ralph's cabled diagnosis on the jaw tumor of the Hmong boy—actinomycosis. Miraculously, I was able to convey it to the mother just minutes before they left our camp for Ban Vinai. Once there, it would have been a needle in the haystack operation to find them. I just happened to drive by as the buses were loading at the detention center. On a hunch, I stopped and climbed aboard a bus. The engine was running and it was about to leave. The boy and his mother were sitting in the very back. I begged a scrap of paper from the bus driver, and scribbled out a referral to the Ban Vinai hospital.

* * *

Delighted to hear that you are not sweating departure plans, and will travel light. Plenty of children's toys are available in Udorn, forty-five minutes away. Ready-made clothing for children is easily available, and almost all clothing—even levis— are easily tailored in Nongkhai. Peanut butter is available locally, just very expensive. We eat mostly "native" and love it. We do all our own marketing and cooking.

* * *

The saga of the Hmong boy with the jaw tumor continues to be full of little miracles. We told you that Ralph's cable came in the nick of time as the bus was about to pull out. Well, the following week, Chester Taylor, the dental surgeon, and his wife Margaret, decided to take a Saturday drive to Ban Vinai (five bumpy hours each way in the pickup) to check on the boy's hospitalization, and to deliver some food and money they had for him and his mother. When he wasn't at the hospital, they knew he would be impossible to find in a camp of 40,000 inmates. They decided to try the camp commander's office, even though it would likely know nothing. En route, they literally bumped into the boy and his mother. For the first time since any of us saw her, the mother broke into a smile. They gave them food and money (it turned out they had neither), and got the boy admitted to the hospital. He should be fine, with time and some treatment.

That evening, an exhausted Margaret told me she

wouldn't make it to the Easter "housechurch" we had planned for the next day. "But tell everyone I've had my miracle today."

* * *

Altogether, this has been a wonderful experience for our family. Even with our raspberry harvest at home, we have never had such a long, consistent period of working together as a family. Erik has written two papers here, and has cultivated a writing talent that neither he nor we had anticipated. Kris has learned the complexities of personnel management in the Day Care Center and the intricacies of VOLAG cooperation (the center is under the aegis of IRC, but CRS pays the Lao staff, and Food for the Hungry provides the lunches). Mali has helped in day care, in feeding on the ward, and has cultivated many Lao and Thai friends. Mark has worked at day care, at Food for the Hungry, and as a play therapist on the ward. We will miss this place.

* * *

The focus here continues to be much more on acute than preventive medicine. Wheels must be reinvented. Do you remember when we started having well child clinics in Vientiane, and what happened to admission rates for diptheria, tetanus, polio, and pertussis . . . and malnutrition? And now we have new colleagues, learning for themselves what we learned. And that's life. Hope to see you soon.

21
Erik's Notes

Water Festival

The Lao call it Pi Mai, the Thai call it Songkran. It is the traditional Lao and Thai New Year's celebration in mid-April. This year it lasted officially from Saturday to Wednesday. But we got an early start on Friday at a ceremony in camp that ended up as a two-hour water fight.

The traditional thing to do is gently to pour water down the back of someone's neck, thus "purifying" them. Of course, the Lao and Thai kids, and kids from anywhere else, go way beyond that.

On Saturday, the Lao doctors and nurses had a New Year's *baci* for all the foreigners. Water throwing began around ten in the morning, and lasted til two.

On Sunday, it never stopped. People lined the streets of Nongkhai, bucket in hand, dousing anyone in sight. People in cars could roll up their windows. But I saw many people on bikes and motorcycles get it right in the face. And nobody got mad.

Along Michai, the mainstreet of Nongkhai, thousands

of people gathered to douse hundreds of buddha images that paraded by, perched on the backs of trucks. When we drove downtown to check the mail, we managed to park about twenty yards from the post office. And in that distance, we and our mail got thoroughly soaked. On the way back, Mark insisted on sitting in the back of the pick-up, and enjoyed being the perfect target all the way home.

At home, the neighborhood kids were waiting. We all doused each other, said thank you and a happy new year, as was proper. Then we agreed to meet again at two-thirty. We got four buckets ready and made about ten water balloons. They came with high-powered squirt guns. We had a great water fight. Then we all went out by the road and splashed everything that came by. It was a real blast!

Nutrition Survey

I had helped Mom with the basic nutrition survey of 200 refugee kids in the outpatient clinic. Now she wanted several comparisons.

First she wondered if there was any difference between the "sick" kids who came to the clinic, and the "normal" kids out in the camp. The Oregon public health team was doing a mass immunization of kids on the South side of the camp. So I was assigned to weigh and measure the kids before they got their shots.

I measured 150 kids. It turned out that 71 percent of them were below the fifth percentile for weight. In our outpatient sample, that figure had been 56 percent. So the normal kids were more malnourished than the sick ones. My dad's theory is that parents who bring their kids to the hospital clinic are more "with it," and would also try harder to feed their kids.

Next, Mom wanted a comparison of the camp kids with those in surrounding Thai villages. So it was arranged that I would go along with Dr. Levi on some of the IRC village health trips to weigh and measure.

Levi drives fast. On our way out of town, we passed Kris, in Steve's truck, on her way to the camp. She waved a whole bunch of Chicklets she had bought for the daycare kids. We drove east, parallel with the Mekong, for about two hours. At Bung Khan, we turned down to the river, to a group of Hmong who had just crossed on Monday. A priest and a nurse were there from CRS (Catholic Relief Services), taking care of cuts and other minor things. We left them some medicines and then stopped in the village for brunch.

It was another fifty kilometers to our village for the day, forty of them on bad roads. We had to detour around three missing bridges.

We set up, as usual, in the temple courtyard. Levi examined the patients, then sent them to the van, where Robby and Ken filled prescriptions, and then I measured and weighed them. I did 87 kids in this village.

The data from this and other villages showed that there was lots of malnutrition among Thai village kids. But the figures were nowhere near as bad as among the kids in the refugee camp.

Nongkhai

What does a person do on a day when he doesn't have to be at work in the camp, and the April temperature is over 100 degrees? One afternoon I got bored with lying under the ceiling fan, and told Dad I was going to ride the bike into town. He thought I was crazy—sun stroke perhaps—and he would have Mom examine me when she got home. But he gave me some errands to do while in town.

A lot of people stared at the *falang*, as if wondering, "what's that *falang* doing on a bicycle? Everyone knows that all *falang* are rich, and ride around in cars." In fact, several months earlier, MIHV had bought bikes for its volunteers, and several other *falang* had now done likewise. But old stereotypes don't die easily.

It was always fun to go downtown. And going on a bike made it more so, even in the heat. From the bike, you could "window shop" at all the open store fronts, and thread your way between ten-wheel trucks and samlars and cycles, and kids and dogs.

I stopped at our favorite grocery shop. It was an open store front about ten feet wide and thirty feet deep, with cluttered shelves on both sides. They didn't have the powdered whole milk I wanted. But they did have packages of stateside spaghetti noodles, at about a dollar a package, which I bought because Dad had promsied to make us a batch of spaghetti for old-times sake.

At the corner store near the river, I could see that they had the milk. But it was sitting on a shelf near the ceiling, and the saleslady seemed helpless to reach for a can. So I climbed up over the merchandise and got it down.

Then I rode to the market. I didn't have a lock along, so I had to walk the bike with me from stall to stall. I bought cabbages, tomatoes, onions, and French bread. It was practically impossible to get all of this loaded on the back of the bike. I ended up with the bread and tomatoes swinging from the handle bars in a plastic bag.

About a mile from home, while I was exchanging jeers with some people in an overloaded bus, the bag broke, and they got the last laugh. I spent about five minutes trying to reload. Finally a sympathetic Thai man came over with a piece of cord. He watched me struggle to tie everything together, and then did it for me. The onlookers waved as I rode off, commenting, no doubt, on the crazy *falang* who didn't know how to carry things home from market.

Futbahn and Takraw

Futbahn is the Thai word for soccer. Every school has a soccer field. The kids in our neighborhood played almost every day, and Mark and I often played with them. They were good players, and we had to work hard to keep from looking like complete fools.

Takraw is harder to define, because I think it is only an Asian game. To an American, it looks vaguely like volleyball, except that you never use your hands. Every other part of your body is used, though, to keep the ball in motion. The ball is woven from bamboo reeds and is a little larger than a softball. Skilled players look like acrobats, flipping themselves upside down to spike a ball over the net with their feet.

In our neighborhood, we had no net, so we just formed a circle and all tried to keep the ball in the air. Mark and I never got to be very good at it, but we loved the game anyway, and the Thai kids like to have some *falang* to play with.

Takraw is the number one sport in Thailand. They'll all tell you that, and you see people playing it everywhere, in the villages and in Bangkok. It is probably also the big game in Laos. In camp, you saw people everywhere tapping away at the ball. I was told that most Asian countries play some variation of Takraw. My dad remembers, as a boy in China, playing a similar game except that, instead of a reed ball, they used copper coins attached to a bunch of feathers.

I'd like to see Takraw become popular in America. Most sports are becoming international. We've exported baseball and frisbee, and finally imported soccer. Maybe Takraw will be next. It's a great game.

Tornado

It was brief, and highly localized. But Mom, who has had first-hand experience with a Fillmore County twister, says we had a tornado in Nongkhai one evening in late April.

Mom and Dad and I were in the bedroom for a book conference. There was a bad thunderstorm outside, but we have lots of them here in April. The lights went out, but that happens often. The other kids were the first to recognize that this one was scary. They came into the bedroom. It was the only room that could be fully closed. The noise was deafening. Wind started seeping up through the floorboards and lifted the linoleum off the floor.

We thought we heard voices outside. Dad opened the door to the living room, and we were almost knocked over by the blast of air. Curtains were flying and water was pouring in. Again we heard shouting. Dad ran to the front door and got it open. There, crouching, was Oei, one of the neighbor kids, and her mother. We pulled them in. Their house had been struck by lightning, and then it had blown away. The rest of their family was still hiding in the ruins.

We waited a few minutes for a break in the wind. Then Dad and the mother ran out to get the rest of the household. There were nine of them, from two families, ranging from a crippled grandmother to a tiny baby. We bundled them up in blankets and towels, and brewed a big pot of hot tea. No one was injured. The men made several forays through the storm to try to rescue valuable items like bicycles. They stayed about an hour, and then went to spend the night with nearby relatives.

Kris and I went with Dad into town, to find our landlord, and to check on damage elsewhere, especially at the refugee camp. But less than a mile from home, the roads were hardly wet. We stopped at the house of the missionaries, the Kaetzels. They had experienced only a light shower. But they agreed to run out to camp to confirm that all was well there. (It was.)

The landlord came out with his family, and checked all around our house for downed wires or other damage. There was none. Our house was made of brick and tile. But we saw sheets of mangled tin roofing from other houses scattered around our yard.

I had trouble sleeping last night. It was strange to have no lights on outside, and to think how miraculous it was that we were in the path of the storm and survived.

We got up at five-thirty this morning, and began bringing back the pieces of our neighbor's house. The roof was completely blown off, and the inside was partially burned. It was lucky it rained, or everything would have burned. By nine o'clock there were neat stacks of lumber and tin in the neighbor's yard, and rebuilding had begun.

I then went home and helped clean up there. Everything was wet, and we laid it out to dry . . . tapes, books, radio, clothes, food, furniture. I worried about the family next door. But I also envied their style. I wished I could rebound so quickly from last night.

22
Thailand Karen

Last fall, in Eden Prairie, we got the Sunday paper and read the headline. "Thailand Opens Borders To All Refugees." Hakon was so moved that he sent a cable to General Kriangsak, then the Prime Minister of Thailand. It read:

OUR FAMILY AND NEIGHBORS APPLAUD YOUR DECISION ADMIT ALL REFUGEES. THAI PEOPLE ASSUMING GRAVE RESPONSIBILITY OF MANKIND. FAMILIES EVERYWHERE SHOWER THAILAND WITH BLESSINGS AND WILLINGNESS TO HELP.

When a relatively poor country of forty million people can accept a million refugees along its borders, and do it with only a minimum of conflict, as Thailand has done, then we know that here is a strong culture.

One of the many fringe benefits of volunteering for the

refugee camps here is the chance to live in Thailand. The Thai and Lao cultures are quite similar. They are calm and delightful people.

The Gracious Thai

One night, shortly after our arrival in Nongkhai, Hakon and I were delayed at the camp hospital until after eight. We had no way to notify the kids, who were home and expecting us hours earlier. When we got home we found that several of the neighbors had come over at dark to stay with our worried children, to offer them food, and to guard them until we arrived.

We had many such experiences with the Thai people in Nongkhai.

The landladies were certainly special. Granted, they expected to gain from the rent, as would landladies everywhere. What differed here was to find so many extra touches of graciousness.

Our landlady would bring us samples of the local delicacies, such as mangoes and sticky rice. When we broke glasses, she refused to let us replace them. We enjoyed numerous chats, sharing our cultures—she with a little English, and I with a little Lao. We became friends. When we left, she brought us hand-embroidered pillow cases, and flowers, and gifts for the children.

The landlady at the Taylor house, where other MIHV volunteers lived, was likewise a rare soul. She went with us to the carnival one memorable evening, guiding our purchases, and riding the Ferris wheel with me. She held my hand.

Both of these lovely ladies had strong husbands. But in

the Thai culture it seemed to be the wife who took responsibility for managing property. Both had built the houses for themselves, but had moved out into cramped quarters when the volunteers came to town and there was a chance to reduce their mortgages through rentals.

On the day after the fire, I was examining a woman with smoke injuries who was temporarily blinded. I decided to hospitalize her. As she lay on the bench outside the OPD, two Thai soldier walked by on the road. I called to them, and asked them to carry the lady into the hospital. I suppose they were surprised at my boldness. They stopped, put down their weapons, and tenderly carried her in.

We knew that the politeness was sometimes an oriental mask. But the only openly unpleasant Thai we met was an occasional *samlar* driver, scrambling for his hard-earned money, seeing the world as hostile and the rich *falang* as an easy touch.

The mother of the lady who cut our hair would come and sit with us whenever we were there. Gracious to a fault, she talked about her nine children, several of whom had emigrated to the United States. Would she ever visit them? "It's better that I work to send them there," she said. She was proud of how well they did in school. She saved all she could to keep them in school as long as possible.

We had the pleasure of numerous meetings with medical faculty members of Khon Kaen University. Dean Netrachaleo Sanpitak is the first woman dean in Thailand, an exceptionally competent and dedicated person. When I was leaving Khon Kaen one evening, for the jerky three-hour train ride back to Nongkhai, she saw me off with a take-out dinner of fried rice to eat on the way. I still have the Thai spoon from that meal—a souvenir of another special touch from the gracious Thai.

Bike Ride

The kids had done it often, but here in April was my first chance to ride beyond our house, and see what lay further down that little dirt road. Mark came along to guide his mother.

Most of the houses in our neighborhood were of the traditional Thai style, built on stilts. There were children, dogs, buffalos, chickens and ducks in abundance under and around the houses.

Beyond the neighborhood, we rode past paddy fields starting to green, then more houses. Some of the children cried "falang." We rode past a pottery factory, we saw fruit trees being mulched, we met motorcycles with several riders and a middle-aged Thai lady riding a bicycle with an enormous market basket.

We rode briefly on pavement, past a beautiful temple and burial ground, then into a tightly settled area with ·many thatched roofs, and flowering trees with purple blooms. Next came the Technical College with its lovely grounds and the scent of blooming frangipani trees ... and a hundred yards further the scent of pig manure, near where a Thai lady sat gracefully on her clean dirt floor ... and then suddenly out onto the main highway.

We turned uphill past the prison with its high concrete walls, then to level ground with rice paddies and buffalos on the right, a few houses and shops on the left, then past the pile of teak logs from Laos that mark the turn-in to our house. And there were Erik and some neighbor children setting off a fire cracker. Mark joined them. And I went to the typewriter.

Buffalos

Of all the sights of Thailand, my own favorite may seem very strange. I like buffalos. It stems, I suppose, from my childhood years of being the one who chased our cows across Highway 16 in southern Minnesota every morning and evening. In Nongkhai, their herd is usually water buffalos, rather than cows, and the one in charge is often a little boy, rather than a little girl.

But when the traffic stops on Friendship Highway, I delight to sit and watch, and I think I know what goes on in the minds of the little boys—and of the animals.

The buffalos change their minds in the middle of the road, or calmly defecate before going on. Today I saw a Thai farm woman pulling with all her might on the rope around the neck of her huge charge— who simply stood there, waiting for us to stop. We did. I think the passing traffic here is kinder than I remember as a girl. The Thai may be reckless drivers, but they do stop for what they call "the inspector general."

I see them in the *klongs* (canals), munching waterlilies, with only their nose and horns above water. I see their bodies gleaming in the moonlight as I return from night rounds. They show no ID to the guards at the camp gate. They wander in and out wherever they choose. One day a calf got into the small space between the hospital and the OPD.

I've asked many Thai why the buffalos are never rustled. Everything else left loose seems to get stolen. It simply isn't done, they say. An average buffalo sells for 2,000 *baht* ($100). Every owner, and all the neighbors, know exactly which buffalo belongs to whom.

I have a secret yearning. It's to ride a buffalo. I see the small kids mounted so elegantly, far back on the animal, and the ponderous beasts responding to a mere touch. I wonder how long it would take me to be so relaxed, and so confident.

On our last Sunday, driving to camp, we saw the buffalos hitched to plows in the rice paddies—their annual day of work, we called it. The sun, the water, and the rich green of the seed rice, etched a beautiful memory. On the way back we saw the buffalos bathing, noses barely above water, and gorgeous flame trees in the background. Next we passed a brigade of white Brahmans parading down the street. We stopped for a red light. Eight white buffalos came toward us, through the red light. The other cars stopped. The buffalos parted around our car, the magnificent bull passing within an inch of our car mirror. Now, there's a memory of Thailand.

23
Last Day Karen

I had finished my last rounds, and Hakon his last English-and-orientation class. We decided to go one more time to the Children's Graveyard, partly to share its pathos with our successors, the Andersons, and partly to reinforce for ourselves the scale of the unfinished business here. The sight overwhelmed us again, as it did the Andersons.

Driving back to town, we noticed some commotion ahead, and saw Souba, one of the male nurses, standing beside the road in hancuffs. We stopped, and Hakon was soon engaged in an earnest conversation with the Thai police officer who had arrested him. Souba was one of Hakon's most faithful students. Last week, when Souba finally got his T-number, he and Hakon had bear-hugged each other in highly non-Asian fashion—in fact Hakon's glasses had gotten broken in the excitement. And now Souba looked pathetic.

Apparently, he and his wife had hitched a ride to town

with the Food for the Hungry volunteers. They had been caught without a pass riding the bus back to camp. Hakon suggested that, since the *falang* had taken these people out, they should also be responsible for bringing them back in to camp. He offered to deliver Souba back to the *falang* who brought him out—or to drive him back to the camp himself. The officer pondered this, and then decided, "You take them back to camp. You're no different from the other falang." Then he told Souba his punishment would be a mere ten push-ups. Souba, who had feared for a month in the cooler, drew himself up, as only a former sargeant could, and swiftly executed his ten push-ups. Then he flashed the officer a crisp thank-you salute, and, with his wife, raced joyously to our truck.

That gave us one more look at the camp, such a dismal looking place, and yet, clearly, the home of powerful dreams. It had been a week of saying good-bye to these people. The Lao doctors had given a farewell *baci*, the epitome of beautiful Lao ceremonies. They had chosen our old friend, the venerable Maha Chanty, to lead the incantations. They had tied *baci* strings on our wrists, and we on their's, and we had wished each other abundant blessings. There had been speeches and gifts and a rich Lao feast (they must have pooled weeks of food allowances), and all this had unfolded in a cramped refugee cubicle that seemed, for the occasion, like a palace.

We hurried home for final packing. It was sobering to see the truck crammed with the gear of six Americans "traveling light." The landlord and his family came by and draped us with garlands of frangipani, and gave each of the children a gift. At the train station that evening, it was overwhelming to find scores of refugee friends seeing us off. They had managed to get out of camp, and we could only hope they would manage to get back in. As we pulled out, one of the day care workers was crying, and chasing the train—an uncharacteristic display of emotion in the old culture, but surely an affirmation that she had bonded with the new culture, and could hardly wait for her own journey to begin. We had been awed by many such expressions during the week.

Twenty years ago, we had bonded, too, with the people of Southeast Asia. During the let-it-all-hang-out phase in our own culture, we had lived here with people who cultivated quiet and calmness in the face of disagreement and conflict. Now we had touched those strengths again—what a privilege to have enjoyed twice in a lifetime.

It was a further privilege, the second time around, to have shared this with our children, to see them stretch their minds into a perspective larger than one culture, and discover new delights—*samlars*, and sticky rice, and peeling green mangoes with the neighbor kids.

Would there be a third time? We would work hard to save up for that. Would it be in a year or two . . . or would we come here with grandchildren, like the Andersons had . . . or with a contingent of naturalized Lao-American volunteer doctors and nurses . . . or would we visit our children in their own overseas endeavors? We could not know.

For now, we would go home to our jobs and our schools, far more aware than before of the strengths of our own culture, and also more aware of how other cultures have and will enrich it.

We are four centuries of refugees. I sing to someone's great-great grandparents, and to my own grandparents, and to my husband. And I sing to Boutsaba, and Nghi, and Sawie, and Bouahong, and all the others. They carry the gift of the refugees.

Conclusion

As first we see refugees only with the eyes of our own culture—as they see us with the eyes of their's.

And then the surprises begin.

About Volunteers

The ideas that the "haves" should help the "have-nots" runs far deeper in our culture than in most. Sometimes, we feel downright guilty about living as well as we do. The image of a poor and helpless-looking refugee can inspire us to generosities like sponsoring a refugee family, or flying off to a refugee camp.

But our experiences, somehow, don't often fit that model. In the case of our family, the thought that we might be doing something sacrificial in Nongkhai vanished in the realization that this was the most enriching experience our family had ever had. Other volunteers had similar reactions. The categories of "haves" and "have-nots" are rarely as simple as a single culture or sub-culture thinks they are.

A volunteer who reaches out to a "disadvantaged" one,

is asserting the worthiness of his own culture. This confidence also allows him to share in the perceptions of the other's culture—and thereby to expand his own. Volunteers lead a rich life.

About Refugees

"The wretched refuse of your teeming shore"— words of Emma Lazarus inscribed in the Statue of Liberty—captures, for most of us, our first impression of refugees.

Our double-take, when we look inside that wrapping, is part of the rich laughter of history. The new world was dismissed as a haven for rebels—who turned out to be patricians recoiling at the new immigrant riff-raff—who turned out to be over-achievers sneering at the clods homesteading westward—who turned out to be giants in the earth— etcetera. (And not a one of them or us would have expected much from a peasant carpenter in Galilee.)

We are as adept as our forefathers at playing straight man to history's little jokes.

Twenty years ago, few of us thought the city of Miami could survive that year's onslaught of refugees from Cuba, who are today the backbone of the city, and almost as alarmed as the rest of us over the latest wave from Cuba.

In recent years, the Southeast Asian refugees have followed the script exactly—and so have we. Already, thousands of them have stepped smartly into the sinews of our society. And we have marshalled an army of volunteers and a growth-industry of publicly-funded resettlement experts and educators and health providers to help these "helpless" people toward self-sufficiency, and to help the rest of us endure this assault on our resources and sensibilities.

The punch line, this time around, could be a gem: Imagine a strong society that for several generations has tried to blur the distinctions between its copers and non-copers. It is now searching for a more compassionate way to organize itself, and for the resolve to make some changes. But there are not as many models of good coping around as there used to be. It could use an infusion of vigorous new blood. And now imagine the least likely place on earth to produce a shot of American frontier mentality—the ancient, oblique, and gentle cultures of Southeast Asia. History can be more fun than fiction.

There is an unbroken family line of vitality and self-selected competence that has enriched the American society in every generation. This bloodline is stronger than race or education or money. It is the family of survivors. Those dazed refugees who just stepped off the plane are direct social descendants of all our earlier immigrant survivors.

Here, by harsh rules of succession, are sons and daughters of the American Revolution.

Here, as unlikely-looking as all their predecessors, are more "giants in the earth."

Here, in its traditional wrapping, is the gift.

Glossary

ACRONYMS
ARC   American Refugee Committee
CRS   Catholic Releif Services
IRC   International Rescue Committee
MIHV   Minnesota International Health Volunteers
OPD   Outpatient Department
UNHCR   United Nations High Commission for Refugees
VOLAG   Voluntary Agency

THAI-LAO WORDS
baci   traditional well-wishing ceremony
baht   Thai currency (20 baht=$1.00)
falang   foreigner
lamvong   classical dance
samlar   three-wheeled pedicab
soon   camp
wat   Buddhist temple